Diary of a foster kid growing up

Diary of a foster kid growing up

T Dog

Copyright © 2019 by T Dog.

Library of Congress Control Number: 2019906211
ISBN: Hardcover 978-1-7960-3788-3
Softcover 978-1-7960-3789-0
eBook 978-1-7960-3803-3

All rights reserved. No part of this book may be reproduced or transmitted in any form or by any means, electronic or mechanical, including photocopying, recording, or by any information storage and retrieval system, without permission in writing from the copyright owner.

Any people depicted in stock imagery provided by Getty Images are models, and such images are being used for illustrative purposes only.
Certain stock imagery © Getty Images.

Print information available on the last page.

Rev. date: 06/11/2019

To order additional copies of this book, contact:
Xlibris
1-888-795-4274
www.Xlibris.com
Orders@Xlibris.com
796867

CONTENTS

Acknowledgement vii

Chapter 1 1
    My Life 3
Chapter 2 33
    Hood Life 35
Chapter 3 39
    Dope Game 41
Chapter 4 45
    Doing Jail Time 47
Chapter 5 59
    Thinking in Prison 61

Acknowledgement

All praise is due to the creator. I thank Him for always coming through for me in time, on time and for all my up's and down's.

To all my kids, always know that daddy love you know matter what.

My brothers, I love ya'll.

My mom, thanks for having me I love you.

To my adopted parent thanks so much for keeping us all in church it really helped. To my foster family I will always love ya'll no matter what and we are still family.

Special thanks to all the book clubs, bookstores and vendors who are always on their grind.

And saving the most important thanks for last, my readers. You are the best; I really do appreciate all the love and support. This one is for you.

Dedicated to my childhood, you made me who I am (struggles).

Chapter 1

My Life

Coming up in this world, I think I was about 8 years old when me and my two other brothers was taken from our mom. We was at school when DCF came and got us at the time. I really don't remember how it felt when we were took. All I know is we never went back to her (mom). As time went on the 3 of us stayed at this one house but, I was too young to know where it was or how to get there. We only stayed there, I would say for only some days. After that was over we all (3 boys) moved to the city to this older lady name Ms. Sherry. She was older but, she still could move around, and she still was able to cook for the three of us. She also had a granddaughter that lived there also. We ate 3 meals a day there. When it was time to play…for me I like hot wheels, the little cars and I would go under this tree out front and play with my cars. She had other family that would come over like her older kids with their kids and one of her daughters had two boys. One was my age and one was older than me but, the one that my age he was cool and that's who I played with at the time. He used to come over and play with me and my hot wheels under the tree, we would make all kinds of roads and bridges for the cars and that was a lot of fun. Now, as I can remember I cannot tell you where my other two brothers were while I played with our foster cousin under the tree (all I know is when it was time to go to these Christmas parties for all the foster kids and my brothers would all be together at the party to see Santa and get gifts. Now, that was fun, and it be a lot of kids out there to get gifts. We got our gifts and took pics then went home. My cousin and me would always play together at the house where I lived. They always came over, so we could play, and I use to love to go to my cousin house. They lived like 30 minutes away from where I lived but it was fun going out there. When I would get out there all we did was play video games and sand lock football but one thing I liked about their house is, it was a 3 bedroom and it was very nice and clean on the inside and out. I never wanted to leave there but, I had too and if I can remember, I use to be mad or sad because I had to go back to where I lived. Not saying where I lived was bad or not clean, I mean it was nice too I just loved to be at my cousin house for some reason. When I did get back home, it might have been a day before we had to go to school. Now, me going to school was not all that bad, all I can remember is we didn't stay too far from school and we had to walk there and that was not all that bad. The name of my school was Phillip Elementary, we lived in the black area, but it was laid back. Nothing bad going on like shooting or a lot of fighting but I do remember this girl that stayed across the street and her name was Lisa. She was pretty to me, I guess you know I tried to get with her lol. I was young but, I did know what pretty was and that was her. One day I asked her to come over and when she did, I tried to kiss her on the lips lol. I do not remember if we did or did not, but I do know I tried. After that, she never really came over like that. I don't know why, maybe I was trying to do too much at a young age I guess…it was dude friends around at the time and one dude that stayed next to us we played football on the side of the house almost every day and that was fun. Now as time went on I cannot recall of me and my own brothers playing together too much but I do remember us having to go to church on Sunday. The preacher would come pick us up because we didn't have a car and I do remember the lady that would come pick us up, so we could go see our mom and dad at the HRS offices, so we could visit them all. All I can say is me and my brothers stayed there with mom and dad for like an hour and then we had to go back to where we lived but, before we left dad would give us $20 apiece. That made us feel pretty good and loved. I think we visit only for a short time before all the visits stopped. Then we all stopped going to see mom and dad. I can't say how it made us feel at the time, all I know is we never went back again, and time went on til one day we were outside just hanggin' out and our foster mom called us to the front door and asked us, "Do we know a lady by the name of Estail Bentley?" Now we were at least 6, 9, and 11 at the time. We started to think for a min and we was like, "I think that is our grandmother, our momma mom." Our foster mom told us she had just passed away and we looked at each other with the sad face...time went on and one other day our foster mom came to us and said, "Our older brother had to go." We did not understand why so my older brother left and went to another foster home. While we stayed there we did not understand why, all we knew he was gone to another home to live. So now, it's just the two of us at this foster home with her granddaughter. Time went on and we lived there for a lil while longer and one day our foster parent came to the two of us and said, "That we were moving too because she was getting too old to keep kids." So, we left too and went to another home. Now we are in the country far from the city part that we use to live at (we are in the woods with trucks and big trucks and a lot more kids around). It's just me and my brother that is two yrs younger than me and his name is Flex and this home where we live at now in the country is a brick house with 4 bedrooms with 4 kids. Two boys, two girls, their mom and dad living there. So now, we are at this new home out in the country and all these woods and other kids. Somewhere new to me and my brother so we get settled in the house and within some months we had to go somewhere with the lady that brought us to the house. She had come to pick us up, so we went with her. Me and my brother and when we got to where we were going, we got out of the car and seen our older brother. I also do not remember how it felt but, we all was there, so we all went in this place and sat down. I think they called us back one at a time to see the doctor, so the doctor took blood from all of us one at a time and after we was done we all went our separate ways. My older brother went back to where he lived and me and my brother that's two years younger than me went back to the country. After some time went on not even a year the same lady came back to get my brother and took him to live with our so call dad but, I could not go. I didn't know why I couldn't go at the time but, I found out that later. Now I am in my new foster home all by myself chillin' with their kids… so I go put my things up in the room where me and the boys are sleeping and come back out to look at T.V. It was a 4-bedroom house and it was a long house. I ask their mom, "What should I call them?" They were like, "You can call me by my name or you can call us mom and dad." I went with mom and dad. So, now I'm locked in my new foster home and all we did was play sand lock football or work. Now the kind of work mom and dad did was fieldwork like peanut field, cutting greens and throwing watermelons. Just all kind of fieldwork (you name it, we did it). Not only did we work in the fields we also helped our dad plant the seeds. While he was on the tractor and when everything came up, we were out there picking and pulling everything up and putting it on the truck, so we could go to the flea market; so, we could sell it. After school, we changed clothes and made our way to work and for some reason that is how we had to make our money, so we could buy our school clothes for school. The sad thing about me doing it was I was good and fast at some of the fieldwork but some of it I was slow to pick a bucket and that was peanuts. It took me all day long to pick a bucket of peanuts and the money I got for picking the peanuts was good for me because when we stopped by the store, I could go in and buy me all the candy and chips I wanted. When it was time to go shop for school clothes and when we got to the stores our mom and dad would go ahead a buy everything for us for school. As I can recall I did dress pretty good back then when I was in school and we did have everything we all needed for school so that was pretty cool with me. I remember one time I had saved up my money, all my money I was making from working in the field and I came home to check my lil piggy bank and when I looked in it all my money was gone. I was mad as hell about that and everybody was looking crazy like they didn't know what had happened but, they knew who had took my money. At the time I was young and too little to even fight about it, so I just let it go. As time went on we kept working in the fields and sometime dad would do it all by himself while we played in the trees climbing them. One day we were about to leave to go home but, before we left we was riding on the back of the truck when I was playing around, and I was on the side of the truck for some reason and I ended up falling off the truck (on the side of the truck) and the tire ran over my knee and it hurt so bad. I was crying and when I told my dad he did not want to believe me, talking about that truck did not run over your leg boy. I was like dang he does not even believe me. Even tho' I was not hurt that bad it still hurt like hell. After that we got home and chilled out, now I must admit I was a little bad back then because I can recall one time we were over to our cousin house and I saw him light a fire work then put it out with his fingers. I was sitting there saying in my head like wow he is not scared to put out fire with his finger. When I got back home we had fireworks home and one day after school I went into our mom and dad room where the fireworks were and grabbed one big one and the reason for me grabbing the big one is because I felt like it would be easier to put out for some reason. I found a lighter and I lit it the first time, but I didn't hold the lighter there long enough, so I did it again. The second time and boi there it was, it lit, and I tried to put it out but when it was lit I was too scared to put my finger on the fire to put it out. So next thing you know it started to pop, pop, pop, pop everywhere in the room. I picked it up and headed for the door with it, so it could finish poppin lol boi that shit was too funny but not funny then when it was done. My dad called me back in the house, so I could get hit with his belt and he was a big guy with a big belt and all he had me to do was hold out my hand and he would hit me like 3 or 4 times in the hand. Let me tell you that shit hurt too. I would jump high as hell and run but he would call me back to him, so he could finish hitting my hand. When he was done, I would run outside or to the room and cry, now that I look back at it that shit was too funny lol. While in school, I was pretty good sometimes when I wasn't mad or in a bad mood because if I was mad or in a bad mood I would have an attitude out this world and be mean to all my teachers. When I wanted to be good I would do good in all my classes and my favorite subject was math. When it started to get harder, I wouldn't like it anymore until my teacher would teach me how to do it then I would like it again. For some reason I stop changing classes like everybody else in school and they just put me in this one class all day. When the bell would ring, we could leave out, but I still had to come back to that one classroom. I guess it was a class for all the bad kids and all the kids that had bad attitudes had to be in this class but, it wasn't that bad being in this class because it was two females in this class that I thought was very pretty. You know me I had to be the one to wanna like them both but, one of them was playing hard to get but she was pretty tho and the other one was cool. She wasn't easy I guess she liked me too in a way to where I would flirt with her a lil bit more in class. In school, we would have like 30 minutes to just read a book of our choice and I would be looking around the book and be looking at her like I was shy or something. She would smile and think I was so fucked up about her because I did that. The reason why I was doing it was to make her laugh really but we would flirt a lot in class as much as we could. She was bad to just like all of us but there was one-man teacher that came to teach our class and I would be mean to him just to see what he would do. He was mean too but not only was he mean his ass was black as hell. I would be mean to him (not call him names or anything) just be hard headed sometimes or l would be late getting back to his classroom or when a subject would get hard in class I would get an attitude. That would make us bump heads in class but overall, he was a pretty good dude. Then for some reason our teachers changed to this real black 5'7" lady (she was real black) her blackness was pretty, and she had a very pretty smile. She was kind of mean too but she was also nice. She had to be mean with kids like us in her class but for some reason I had to try her too, just to see how far I could go with her. It was not too far but she did care for us a lot I can say. She would take her time and help us with our work and we would be bad, until one day I came to school with a different attitude and looked at her different and wanted to be nice to her and ever since then we were tighter than anything in the world. She was like a mom to me and she showed me so much love til at some point I felt like she was my mom til I had to go home to my foster parents. At some point in my life, being there my real mom had my little brother and once foster care (I guess) found out they took him too. Then he was there staying with us at the house as a little boy and as time went by I got tired of being there with my foster parents til one day I went to school and told my teacher I didn't wanna go back home. I was scared to say anything because I didn't know what happened if I told someone that we were getting beatings and I wanted me and my brother to move because we didn't wanna stay there anymore. It was all a blessing because when I did say something we never made it back to their house. They took us to the HRS office, they took us in a room and had us to take off our shirt, and my lil brother had whaps on him so when they got to me to take my shirt off, I had an attitude because now I was scared of what they would do. I still took mine off, they looked at my body, they did not let us go back, and in that same day, we had another foster parent there to pick us up. Now the whole time my brother and me was sitting up to the HRS office I was saying to myself, "I hope we get better parents then the last home." One or two hours had passed, and a lady came while we were in the back waiting, when we came out to meet her I looked up and was like 'wow' she is pretty, and she dress very nice. My lil brother and I followed her, so we could go outside. She was riding in a nice car; it was a Mercedes Benz. It was an old one, but it was clean. She had her sister in the car waiting, so we left and was on our way to our new home. My brother and I rode with our new foster mom and her sister to our new house; we made one stop before we got home to pick up this girl. She was older; she looked like she was older than my brother and me. She got in and we headed to our new home. As we were riding, I was looking trying to see where we were at and how to get to where we were going. It started to get dark, but I still could see, I just never been in this area before. We dropped off her sister and the girl that was sitting in the back seat with me and my brother after they got out we rode down this road to our foster mom house and it had a big fence around it and the house was pretty big. We got out me and my little brother with our book bag and walk in the house it was very nice on the inside. I said to myself, "Thank you Lord we have hit jackpot" and we did. The lady took us back to where we were sleeping at and as we were walking we passed rooms as well and when I looked in them they were all real clean like no one slept in them. Then we go to the room where we were going to sleep, and this room was so clean all you seen was two twin beds that had Little Mermaids covers on them. I was like 'wow' this is it, so we put our stuff down and then we walked back in the kitchen were the lady was. I think she fried us some chicken to eat so as she was cooking I asked her, "what do you want us to call you" and she said, "you can call me Ms. Susie, or you can call me Grandma like my little Granddaughter do" so I said, "We'll call you Grandma." She was cool with that…After we ate I noticed we only had our book bags and no clothes to go to school in because they took us out of school and we never went back to our old house. All we had was the one outfit we had on and that was it but, the lady made a way for us. She gave me one of her outfits out her closet, it was very colorful, but it looked like someone had ironed it for some hours. When I got up for school the next morning, I put the outfit on; it was too big, so she gave me a belt, or I already had one, so I put the belt on my shorts. I then put the button-down shirt on and buttoned it up and you could not even tell it was too big at all. Not only that back then the style was to wear big clothes like that, so I was Gucci. She told me where the bus stop was at and I got on the bus (I was only in middle school at the time). We got to school and I'm feelin like new money…I got my new fit and feeling good about our new home. I'm in school chillin and after school was over all the kids had to walk to their busses. I had a new bus this time because I didn't stay in the same place, so I got on this new bus with all white kids and two mixed kids. You know I sat by the mix boy and the kids noticed a new kid on the bus and that was me. I'm black you can't help but to see me because I'm the only one on the bus this color. Next thing you know some kid yelled out, "Hey, nigger you going to pick cotton today!" I was about to say something but the mix dude beside me told me, "Just chill they always act like that" but I'm saying to myself, "If I have to keep riding this bus with these crackers saying shit like this imma be in some trouble." As we are riding, we got to my bus stop but I'm saying to myself, "this is not where I got on this morning," but I got off the bus anyway and this white dude got off with me, but he was cool tho. He somehow had a bike and told me he would take me home. He asked me, "Do I know where I stayed?" and I told him, "Yea." I got on the handle bars and I showed him where the house was. He dropped me off and I told him, "Thanks," then he pulled off. I walked in the yard and said to myself, "Wow, I made it back here even tho it was dark when I got here." When I got in the house, I told my grandma the school put me on the wrong bus after school was out and it was an all-white bus and the white kids was calling me names and stuff. She was like I'm sorry to hear that, but I see you found your way back home. I was like, yes, I had to and one of the white boys from the bus brought me here on his bike. While my brother and I was staying there, it was nice, but I can say this I still had a bad attitude as a child. I do not know why, I just did. Not only did I have a bad attitude my lil brother was bad as well. He would get home before me and I would go to our room to take off my school clothes and put down my book bag but when I would get to our room, my lil brother done fucked up the whole room and when I say the whole, I mean the whole room. I do not know why he would do it, but he did and that went on for some days after we would clean the room up. I used to be mad as hell with him for messing up the room like he did because I was always this clean guy and he wanna come mess things up just to be bad. After that grandma gave me my own room and I was happy for that with my own TV. I stayed in my room a lot looking at TV or talking on the phone and really the only time I would come out was to fry some chicken or just eat or go play basketball with our foster cousin next door. After staying there for a year or more, I seen that this is the last home for me and my brother to move to, so we need to be and stay good, so we don't have to move to another foster home. What I did was ask our grandma, "Can our big brother come stay here with us?" and she said, "Yes." It did not take my brother long to get there with us at grandma house. I was happy we all was happy about our big brother being there, the only thing I didn't know was did he like it here or did he miss his old home. He stayed in the city and we was still in the country but just not that far in the woods as we use to be. Where we stayed this time was closer to the city, so everybody wasn't that country then the last home we stayed at. My grandma had style and could dress and loved nice cars, her house was big and clean. She always cleaned up and she always told us after we got home to take off our school clothes before we went out to play and that is what we did. After my big brother was there with us for some months came our real mom came by to visit us and the dude we called dad was with her, they talked with us and my grandma came out the door and my real mom and grandma was talking, and I saw my mom hug my grandma. Come to find out grandma told my mom, she would never keep her kids away from her and that our mom and dad could come see us anytime. She wanted to but, that was the last time mom and dad came out there to see us there. As time went on one day, grandma came and asked us, "Did we want to stay there for good?" and we all said, "Yes." And, on top of us staying their grandma had another child come move with us and she was a lot younger then we all was, but I guess it was something about the lil girl that grandma loved. She could not talk but what grandma did was she adopted all of us as her own children and she asked us did we want our name changed to her last name and we all said yes. Time went on and one day I asked my brother why he had to move way back when we all we all was together, and he told me that the lil girl that stayed with us lied and said that he touched her in the wrong way. That's why he had to move to another home, I was mad that, that girl had lied on my brother, but we were back together again at one big house. Now we all staying there for some time now and I wanted to be the smart guy to see if this lady we call grandma really loved us. So, what I did was sometimes I would be bad in school and she would have to come get me and she hated that but what really made everybody mad was one day they could not find me. The only person knew where I was, was my big brother but everybody was looking for me trying to see where I was. They could not find me, but I was right there under their noses. I was in the next room to them listening to everything they were saying about me and all I could hear was he gone have to move because he ain't finna have my mom stressed out. Everybody was talking shit and then I heard my brother walking up and down the hallway and they asking him way I'm at but at first my brother didn't wanna say nothing. When they started to say, "Well if he doesn't get back here within the next hour or so we calling the police to come find him." So, what my brother did was started talking loud saying, "boi you gone have to come out because we gone have to leave if you don't and I don't wanna leave." After I heard that I came out of the closet in the last room and when I walked pass I said, "I didn't even run away, I was in the room." The reason I was doing this was to see if our grandma really cared about us. Her kids at the time was only her two girls, one stayed there and the other came from the city from time to time but the daughter from the city was one of the girls I really didn't care for like that. The way I seen her is she thought she was all that and she was red, so she really thought she was the shit plus she didn't stay here so she was in her all that mood and that mood I love my mom and these foster kids ain't finna kill my momma because they wanna run away. The daughter that stayed there with us was cool and that is the room I was in the whole time, but she was really cool. All she like to do was go to church, dress, listen to church music. Sometimes we would get into it about somethings like when she wanted us to go to her church and we was not with it. She had company over to the house one day and she was talking about I was going to church and I was like, "no, I'm not" and this girl slapped me in the face and I just pushed her into the wall. Our grandma came back where we was to see what was going on but before grandma came back there I was finna do something to her ass lol but overall she was a very cool sister I never had. She could cook, she would sing, and she would let me drive her car. At one point, she was going to let me have one of her cars she had until one day I was coming from getting a haircut and had a car full. My older brother was on the back of the car on my side and as I was backing up he jumped off the car without letting me know that it was a pole behind me. I ended up hitting the pole on my side of the door. That is how I ended up not getting that car from my sister. I think I was about 16 or 17 years old. I remember being in my room one day and this dude tall and dark skin come bustin in my room and it was grandma nephew, he was coming out of the army. At first, we did not get alone but after some time we ended up being pretty cool. He would come get me and we would ride and talk about everything, but he would really do all the talking and I would stay up listening to him while he drove to wherever we was going. Two things we did have in common was we was 100% real and we both love women. Everywhere we would go we would holla at females and not only that we would talk them into doing whatever it was we wanted them to do and that was have sex with the both of us. If there was a female that I could not have, and he could have then I would fall back and let cuz do his thing or I would be in the closet and she not knowing it watching cuz get that pussy. All I would be doing is laughing but cuz was like ten years older than me, but he loved to hang out with me. He loved teaching and putting me up on game about everything, life, people, women guns and just being by yourself is the best because you don't have to worry about these so call friends in your face. I have a lot of love and respect for him and he always would tell me cuz you smarter than you think you is and he always stuck in my head as time went on. I had to think on that every chance I got. As time went on staying with my grandma was nice we always went to church on Sundays, grandma got me, and my other two brothers baptized at the church so now we are a part of the church now. Me and my older brother started as an usher for some time opening the door for people as they came in or had to go to the bathroom and maybe after a year we started singing in the choir. That was lots of fun because we had to lead songs. When it was time to take up offering everybody loved to see my older brother marched. While we all sing marching around the church to put our money on the table, my thing was I use to love to sing. I would lead songs and all, my grandma used to love it we use to have the church jumping and after church, we would go across the street and play sand lock football with all the kids that was in church or down the road whoever wanted to play could play. Even older dudes that was from where we are from would stop and play and it was so much fun, after that we would go home, eat Sunday dinner, and chill. While staying at my grandma it was a lot going on, one thing was all the girls of her family loved the shit out of me. I don't know if it was because I was new, or I was cute all I know is I was hot, and I was ready to take as many girls I could down through there. First, grandma use to work at night to the prison and she would leave at 11:00 at night. One afternoon we were all outside playing around and this car pulled up in the yard and this girl got out and guess who she was one of the girls from my class from middle school that I use to flirt with in class. She got out the car and I'm saying to myself like oh shit it is finna go down. Grandma go greet the older lady and come to find out grandma is keeping this girl too so I'm like oh shit I'm finna be in here fucking the shit out of this girl. While they all was talking I just played it cool, so grandma would not know not a thing about me knowing her. The girl could stay and the first night grandma went to work I went to her room and next thing you know we was going at it like every night and being that I had already liked her our sex was even better. I mean the pussy was good and we did that for some months, then she moved to another home, but I never recall having unprotected sex with her. I always used a rubber but that was not the only female grandma let stay there. It was another female that came to stay and we all got the pussy, it was like she was a hoe. So, we all fucked her, me, my brother, my cousin next door (everybody) got that pussy and she was the shit for that if you ask me. I had my share of the females from around my way while I was living there with my grandma cause that's when I got the most pussy. I mean all the girls liked the shit out of me and the only ones I did not and was not going to have sex with was the younger girls. They all liked me too, but I was never the type of dude to like girls that was younger than I was like that it was never a turn on for me. It was not because I thought of jail; I just never liked younger girls. I always liked girls older because I felt like they could handle me like I needed them to but younger was like kids and I don't play like that. Older girls I had them I mean all the girls wanted a piece of me and I gave it to them, some use to like me a lot and would get mad because I had their cousin on my joc all at the same time, but I didn't care because I was fuckin. I remember somehow, I ended up seeing one of the girls from my old foster home that I use to live at and she was feeling me so bad til she stole her mom car one night to come give me some pussy. I fucked her good and sent her back on her way, come to find out the girl end up getting in a wreck going back home. I guess she fell asleep on the wheel, but I didn't care because when I use to stay with them she use to get on my last nerves and she was only one or two years younger than me. When I moved, and we saw each other again what came to my mind was imam fuck her for payback and that is what I did. It was a lot going down at my grandma house. I remember one day I was in my room doing something like talking on the phone or looking at TV and my grandma called me to the kitchen and when I walked in there, I see my grandma and my niece God daddy. So, I'm standing up there and God daddy asked me was I or have I had sex with their or his Goddaughter lol it's funny to me how they wanted to try this foster kid with some bullshit like this. I said, "No" and then I said, "why yall asking me why not ask her." This is what dude said we wanted to come ask you because we know all the lil girls like you around here, so we came to you. I said to myself, "Look at this shit they think I'm that slow to where I'll tell on myself or tell them something." I did not do but they call my niece in the kitchen and asked her, and she looked at them crazy and said, "No!" After that, I just walked away back to my room saying to myself, "Way the real love at." They think I am crazy to put my hands on a little girl just because all the girls like me around here, they must be fuckin crazy. I did not get down like that baby, but my thing is how could they try me like that when grandma knew who I be with all the time and that was her nephew, my cousin. We stayed riding and never once have anybody seen me messing with the younger girls I think they wanted to just try to see if I was that crazy to say yea, 'I be fucking her like every night and she love me, ask her lol." I was not tho but after that, it started to make me feel some type of way about them like grandma did not really love us like that for her to come at me like she did. I felt like if your real son was staying here with you, would you have tried him the same way. Fuck no, I am your real son too so why try me like that then, shiit got me fucked up. Living there was not all that bad or all that good, I mean grandma took us out of town and stuff to shop or to theme parks and we would get in trouble there too. I remember one time we stole some wheelchairs and the police had to chase us down to get them back and told us we could not come back for the rest of the year.

I remember being in High School and this dude wanted to fight my older brother because my brother pulled the seat from under him because dude was in my brother seat, well dude wanted to fight but at the time I wasn't there so somebody had to come get me. When I got their dude was standing in front of my brother asking him to fight him, but my brother was like, "No, I'm good and as I got close I was telling my brother to hit his ass bro and next thing you know I seen the dude brother coming behind me. All I did was turned and grabbed dude and slammed him to the ground. That is when everybody started to fight and that day me and my brother got expelled for the whole year. We had to go to a bad school for that year, which was 10th grade. My 9th grade year I remember having this very pretty red girlfriend and we did not have a car to see each other so we would talk on the phone all day and all night as much as we could. I would have her to wear a dress to school, so we could have sex somewhere at school. What I would have her to do was come by my classroom like she had to go to the bathroom and when I seen her walk by I would ask my teacher can I go to the bathroom. I would come out and have her to come to the bathroom and I would have sex with her right there on the floor, then we would get dress and go back to class. We did that at least ten times and the sex was great in there on the floor shiit!! And one time I seen her come by my class, so we could go to the bathroom and I saw her slip and fall, and that shit was too funny lol, so we came out of class to go meet but this time was a bad day for us. After we had this good sex session and I nut real good and I get ready to leave out of the bathroom I look around and I see a teacher and I was stuck. I was finna run but I could not leave my lil lady, so I stayed and we all went to the office and her mom came to pick her up and my grandma came to pick me up, but her mom was mad as hell with me. She did not want us to talk no more her mom came to my house to tell my grandma that she did not want us to talk no more and boy was I mad, I was so mad I cried after they left. What a sad day for me that day. That is one of the girls I really liked in school but it sure was not the last. When I came back to public school my 11th grade year, one day my cousin came by the house and he asked me did I wanna ride to a block party and I told him yea let's do it. He left and came back to get me after we got dress and we went to the party. I only went to get out the house cause where he said he was going I didn't never heard of the place. So, we rode out there, when we got there it was a nice lil crowd out there chilling and listening to music (my cousin) left to go talk to his friends and left my ass to the car chillin. So, I got out the car and just sat by the car and watched all the cars roll through. I didn't know nobody, so I stayed by my cuzin car, after some time some girls came to the car asking who I was, so I told them, and they were feeling a nigga. This one girl was feeling me a whole lot more than the others, I could tell. We talked, and she was being nice and shit, so I was feeling her too. She was tall dark skin and had a very nice shape with a pretty smile. I got her number and called her later, so we could get to know each other, and we did that. We stayed on the phone all the time talking, I would have her on the phone playing with that pussy and I would be rubbin my dick wishing I was right there with her, but we had to wait til the next time we seen each other for us to have each other the way we wanted. That day did come, and I started going to her house and she lived with her mom, dad and two brothers. I went out there to meet her mom and dad to see if everything was good and it was. Her mom and brothers like me, and her dad and I spoke but never really talked that much. When I would come over he would just speak and go in his way. The mom would sit there to get to know me then I would leave. After some time, her mom and dad started to bring her to my house on the weekends, so we could chill for the day. My grandma loved her, so she didn't mind her comin over, so she would come in the house and talk to grandma for a little while. Then I would take her to my room, so we could watch TV and after I knew grandma wasn't comin back there to mess with us is when we would have sex. This was my girlfriend and her pussy was so good to a nigga, I use to be in love with this girl and she was real crazy about me. We would have sex first when she got to my house then I would go cook us some chicken to eat, then we would take a walk or get mad at each other, then before she left we would have sex again. The only thing was she would not let me nut in that pussy (both times). One time I would have to use a rubber, so the last time because the first time I had to feel her and after that it would be bout night time, so after we would have sex for the last time I would call my cousin to come take her back home. When we got to her house I would let her out and I would give her a hug and a kiss, then I would leave. Me and her stayed together for a year or two.

When I got out of school but while in school and me going to the bad school, I would meet other cool kids like myself and we would link up and be friends. My cousin was the one that I use to ride with all the time. He used to work at the Youth Center, so either I would ride with him there or get dropped off and sometimes it would be other kids up there my age or younger, but one day I was upstairs playing basketball and the kid dude one year older than me was up there and he could play basketball good. He was black, but not that black and we played for a lil bit but after he pulled out from his nuts a bag and it contained some little what seem to be white rocks from his nuts. Now at the time I didn't know what it was but he told me I get money, and this right here will make you a lot of money but that shit went in one ear and out the other because at the time I didn't know what that was and didn't really care to know. As time went on me and the dude stayed in touch with each other and when it was time for me to graduate from high school he came so I could ride with him. He was on the side line making me laugh calling my name all loud, but I can say he really made me feel good. My mom and my auntee came with some of my real cousins. I stopped and gave them all a hug after my class tossed our hats in the air. It was a good day for me that day I was happy everybody came. The ones I seen but one person was missing from the scene that I didn't see there and one of them was my cousin that I always ride with. He wasn't there, and I found out later why he didn't come but that's not all. After I got back home from with my homeboy, I came in the house and seen my grandma and asked her why she didn't come to my graduation and she told me that she was there. Now I know she get off work at like 8:00 am but she had enough time to make it so when she was there I said why didn't I see you there but all she said was, "I was there", to me the fucked-up part about it is I didn't see her nowhere around not even to give me a hug of a gift. The year of 2000 was my year and even tho she said she came I didn't see her. It really didn't matter to me then because I still had lots of love there, so I was still blessed, because my real mom and real family was there plus my homie but when our foster sister graduated from the same school everybody from the family was there to see it even me. One thing about me I was going too come because she is considered as my lil sister and before I got there I stopped by a store and picked up a lil gift that would make her smile, I got that gift and was on my way. I got there and made sure she seen me, I was standing on the side line yelling her name til she seen me. After that and it was all over, and all the kids was leaving I followed her to where she was going, she was going where the rest of the family was waiting on her and everybody was taking pics. I waited til it was my turn and gave my sister her gift and a big hug. She told me thank you and we took pics to top it off, now if grandma could make it there why couldn't she make it to mine, for some reason that shit really had me thinking to myself hard as hell. I really felt like this lady don't really love us, I mean she showed loved for letting us stay with her and taking care of us but to me I was missing the most important thing and that was love. I want to feel loved not just one of the foster kids that she just took care of or stayed with her. I wanted real love and I was not feeling that from none of them but before all this had happened it was my last year in school and I was about to be done. Before I was done I ended up getting in a fight on the bus and I guess you know what happened with that, grandma wanted me out the house…what the fuck! It's like a nigga can't ever get in trouble in her house because it would or did make her look bad (it's what I thought). She let me and my older brother move in the trailer down the road by our self but the thing about that is her crazy brother use to or still was staying there so he would still pop up there and be mean to a nigga and I wasn't feeling that at all…this dude was mean and would look at you crazy but what I think what was happening with him is his wife had left him and left him there with that damn lol. I guess grandma brought the trailer but he would still come there or pop up to check things out and when he did I was always there in the room just laying there wishing on a star and sometime when I knew he wasn't coming back I would get a girl to come over there so I could get me some pussy. I would say after a year maybe I left and went to stay with my homeboy, his mom, and his little sister all in a two-bedroom apartment. We all lived there and that's when another chapter of my life started…I'm in the hood!

Me being in the hood never was a place I thought I would be but one thing I did know was when I lived with my grandma and we would ride by this place we call the hood (where I now lived at) I would look down into this one way end, one way out place and see so many black people and it just looked a place where if you go in it, it would be hard to get out because you gone have to shoot your way out of this place but now I live here with my homeboy and his fam...His mom was cool and his two sisters, I even looked at them like they were my sisters too and his mom I looked at her like a mom but I called her by her name and she was cool with that. While I was staying there I remember me and my homie riding and we stopped to get something to eat (now I'm from the country and my homie from town), when we stopped to get something to eat I seen this red girl in the window, so I tapped my homie and asked him, "Aye, bro who is that?" He told me, so I'm like you know her and he said, "yea, I know her." I told him, "Aye, you gotta hook me up bro, I want her my nigga, she is pretty." He told her right then...he was like my bro wanna holla at you and she was like who is your brother and he was like right here in the car with me. She looked off in the car and seen me and was like tell him to call me and gave my homie the number but what she did was said the number out loud, so I could hear it and boi when she did that I said that number over in my head like so many times, so I would not forget it and I didn't. I got back to the hood and wrote it down and called her sometime later. I hit her up one night she was home bout sleep, her and her son and I was trying to get over there to her this night. My homeboy had done left the car to the house because he was charging up the battery, so I was good but what I did to get over there was I called her and told her that I was broke down on the side of the road, but I was right down the road from her house and I wanted to come see her. She told me, "Yea you can stop by," so what I did was let the battery charge up for a lil bit more and was on my way to her house. She stayed with her mom, dad and other two sisters so she had me come to her bedroom window and that's what I did. When I got to the window she let me in and I sat there with her for a minute but having sex with her was the main thing on my mind this night, but I played it cool, but she ended up letting me feel her this night and ever since then she was crazy about me.

That was the first female I moved with after I had her comin in the hood to see me and me having sex with her all over the place. I would sex her all in the car, the bathroom at my house where I was living at with my homeboy and his fam. I was getting that pussy as much as I could. After some time, I had her to get a place but I told her if I move in she can't be trying to kick a nigga out when she get mad and shit because I have too much shit to packing up to move… shiit every chance she got she was on that kick out shit and I got to the point where I would not leave because I didn't wanna move back in with my homeboy peoples. What she did was call the police on me but before they could get me I had done left the apartment. One time she gave them my number and they fucking called me on my cell, so I picked up and the police knew who I was because I use to stay with his grandma back in the days, so he knew who I was, and he tells me I might as well come back cause if I don't it will be a warrant for you, so I came back and went to jail. When I got out I went back to her and we got along a lil bit then she got mad again at me but tried to cut me with a knife and someone else called the police and this time she goes to jail, and I'm stuck to the apartment with her son and younger sister. Now me being the man I am I didn't let her stay I made sure she got out and dropped the charges but while she was gone (sitting in jail) her sister was all over me and wanted me to have sex with her bad and not only that her sister was younger than me. Their mom didn't like me because I was living in the hood, so it was crazy at the house that night but I'm telling the sister no, but she kept trying and I kept telling her no then somehow, I went to sleep but when I woke up the little sister was laying right up under me…I was like damn this girl is trippin so I got up and move abd let her sleep. I would say me, and this female ended up working things out, so I stayed there with her and her lil son and I got along real good.

After some time one day I asked her would she have my baby. She said, "yea," and I never thought she would keep the kid away from me as much as she did. After about a year I moved out to my own place this time and she started to come spend the night over with me with the kids. I was cool with it because I still had love for her. I will let her but after some time we was done things went to getting worse with us and I moved on and by this time I was selling dope and getting money so, I didn't care no more if we would talk or what. As long as I could see my son, but she had other plans for me. She started liking a dude that was hangin' out with me that cool with my so called best-friend.

The reason I'm going to say so called is because I know my home-boy knew he was fucking with my baby momma but they just ain't want to tell me. One day I asked the dude was he fucking her, and the nigga told me yea he is fucking her. Being the cool dude, I am, I wasn't mad I just wanted to know so I could stop fucking with her like that. I mean to me we weren't together anyway because when I moved out to me it was over then. While she was coming over I would still fuck so that's why I wanted to know, shiit she ain't finna give me know STD. I kept it "G" and tell them that it didn't make me mad. She started letting dude bring me my son shiit I didn't care as long as I got to see my son. After that didn't make me mad she stop letting me see my son all over again. I mean dude even wanted to fight me one night in the club about her. One thing about Lil Daddy and that's me is I don't fight over some shit I'm over and done with shiit how I see it she gone do yo ass the same way homie, just wait and see. The night he tried to fight me I was on my shit, I felt like the club was mine. I had nothing but big faces in my pocket and I could get another female like it was nothing, so you can have her homie. I been had her, put a baby in her, treated her good and bad sometimes, so to me ya'll aint doing shit. Dude got mad cause I pulled out a pocket full of big faces. I was showing him I get money, I don't beef about a beef I know love me. I can have her again just wait and see and that is what I did. After they got together he started to get money and she went to tricking on her, so I was there for her and let her come to my place.

At this point I had a new place and a new lady and my lady friend would do anything to make me happy so what I did was one night I asked my lady friend and baby momma would they give me a three-some and they both agreed. Baby momma came to my apartment with a cup in her hand (ready). She had her cup, so she could be loose, as they get dressed and something sexy and when they came out each room they both had on the same sexy outfit. That night the girls wanted the lights out, so I didn't get to see the three-some with them that night and when it was over baby momma left, while my chic stayed there with me coolin like a boss. That's how all my lil ladies' friends made me feel at all times. I tried to be cool with baby momma, but she had something against me about something. I tried being her friend and even tried to be there even when she got her new boyfriend. They got married but I tried with her but it's only one thing I think it could be and that is she's still fucked up about me. After being in and out of my son's life for twelve years because of her she decides to change his last name to her madam last name. At first, I was like hell no but one day my son had called me to come to his football game and at this time I didn't have a car, but I did have a bike. He called me off his mom new husband phone the night before to ask me to come to the game and my son told me that the game start at 8:00 am, so I told him I will be there. I woke up that morning and rode my bike like eight to ten miles, so I could get to his game on time but when I got there I didn't see my son or his mom. I parked my bike and waited for a while and that's when I see my son walking up, I greeted the new husband and I asked him where my son is, so he showed me. I went over to greet my son with a hug and asked him, "do he want to change his last name" and he told me, "yes sir" but the way he said it I could tell he really ain't want to do it and at home I feel like his mom and brother was making him feel left out. I asked him why he wanted to change his last name and he told me because he was the only one in the house with that last name and I told him that's because everybody in his house has different dads that's why. After we had our lil talk it was time to start the game, so I stood there for a minute to watch the game, then I see his mom walking up with her lil girl following her. The lil girl seen me before so she looked at me and I could tell by the way my baby momma was walking it was something up with me being there and it was. I wanted to show my son that I would come anytime he call me and I did. I spoke to her and she spoke back then we went down to watch the game, then I noticed her husband standing at the fence by the team and seen my son mad because he missed a tackle. I go to fence to tell him it's cool your team is already winning so you don't have to be mad if you miss a tackle. It's just a game next time just try harder, but I don't think he was hearing me, but he still told me yes sir. They won the game and it's was time to go for me, so I told him I was about to leave, and he gave him a hug and got on my bike and left. As I'm riding my bike I'm thinking to myself like what is really going on?

Damn, she done got in my son head making him feel like it's better to have her last name then to have his dad last name. Oh well, imma play it how it goes if they want it like that then imma give it to them. I mean it's not like I don't care but she is trying to do too much to try to get at me or make me mad. You know what imma do, imma give her what she wants and when my son gets 18 years old he can change it back if he wants too if not he can keep it the same as his mom. All I know is I tried my best to be a part of his life but of course she wanted to make it hard so imma let her have the fight she wants to win.

Time go on and me and 1st baby momma is done, and life is going on and I'm livin. I'm getting money me and my homie, we fixin up cars and we can have just about any female we want in our city. Me and my homie end up getting our own place now, we supposed to be real bachelors but this female he got staying to the house too much for me, I mean she supposed to stay for a day or two and go home but stayed there with us. I didn't say nothing about it till she started washing clothes like every day and our light bill came and my home boy wanted me to still go half on the bill, now he make way more than me and his lady stayed to the house way more than all of us, so I'm like aye bro she need to go cause she doin too much and I have to pay for it but he still let her be there doin her one two. I chilled and still payed my half but what she started to do was start fuckin mw up with my lady friends cause my homie was doin too much for her, like fuckin with other chicks and she would find out about it or she had to stay to the house the whole time while we were out getting money and she didn't have a car, so she was stuck like chuck with just a phone. When I did let one of my chicks come over to stay that was her chance to talk to them and find out as much as she could and tell on me about having other chicks over to the crib. After I got tired of it I was ready to moveout on my own and see my own lady walk around in nothing or something sexy shiit, I wanted my own and that's what I got. Me and my homie still was friends, but I had to go. At the time I had this fine lil red chick on my team that was really fucked up about me and she would do anything for a nigga shiit I feel like she loved me like no other female I've meet. I mean she would do anything to please me, so what I did I had her to get my own place in her name and she did it with no problem and she let me have it all to myself. She wasn't with no T Dog I ain't doin it because you gone have all them girls over there and imma have to do something to you, she just let me do me and that's' what I did. When I got in my place I had everything like all the females I wanted. My apartment had nothing in the front room at the time only my TV, some DVDS. My bedroom had it all I had so many clothes, shoes, and hats to match, not only that my whole apartment was very clean cause I was a clean person. I said I would get my front room set later and that's what I did, I only had a black recliner in the living room and that was for my company. They can have the chair while I sit on the floor. I would cook when my company came over and everything. I had a box Chevy that was candy apple red with some 24's, 6 twelves and a lil slider that could ride in when I didn't wanna ride in my box. My box use to get me in trouble some time tho cause I would bring it out and I didn't have no DL's at all but still drove and one time my aunt wanted me to take them for a ride in it one day through the hood, so I did and I had the music up loud but when you don't have no DL's you stay looking in your mirrors to see if the cops gone get behind you and this day I was giving them a ride and a cop got behind me because of my oud music. I told my aunt that I was finna jump out and run and as soon as I got to one of my cousins' house, I put the car in park and I ran for it. I ran behind the house jumped a fence then jumped another fence that's when the barbwire got ahold of my clothes and I was stuck for a minute, but I still got away. I ran to a house where I know my mom be at in the hood to hide out and as soon as I get there my mom come out the door, so she helped me change clothes. I got another one of my cousins to take me home but that wasn't the last time I had to run for it. I had to run all the time because I stayed driving and sometimes I would go to jail, but I would go to jail before I use to run. When I started to run I always got away but like I said I had it all friends, stayed around me, I stayed in the club taking pics, all the nigga that was around me was all getting money, we were all ballin and not only that I was so happy til I didn't even know what hatin was because everybody acted like they loved me.

One day I was home countin my money and one of my homeboys was over to my house and I showed him my racks I had saved up, so he told me aye man let me act like your money is mine and I want you to video tape me holding it. I didn't think nothing of it and did it, it was about $22,000 there and about 2 or 3 days I was going to catch a zap and I had this female in the house with me and I told her I would be back so she stayed to my house while I left so, I left out and I see 3 dudes in all black comin after me so I ran back upstairs to try to unlock my door but I had to remember the girl was in the house. I couldn't just go in the house like that and put her in danger and besides they came for me and not her. By the time I got back up to my door to unlock it the girl had unlocked the door because I guess she heard me comin back up to the door, so she opened the door and when I seen her do that I just turned around and punched one of the dudes in the face. While me and the dude was fighting one dude ran in the apartment where the female was, and one dude stayed down the steps for a look out. I was punching and yelling all at the same time and I was giving dude a run for his money this night and he had a big gun in his hand. As I'm punching and screaming he hit me with the gun on the head, so I yelled more, and I punched him, then we started tussling and the one dude that ran in the apartment ran out where we were fighting and swung at me and said, "where it's at." I ducked the punch and he hit my next-door neighbor door and then stood in front of me and fired a shot but in the mist of me and the dude fighting I ended up snatching the dude mask off and I knew who it was, so after the dudes standing the dude I was fighting kept saying shoot that nigga cuz, shoot him but like I say he just fired a shot by my head and then they left. A few minutes later the cops came but I didn't call them and was asking me what happened, and I told them. I think some dudes was trying to rob me, but I don't know. They asked me did I know who it was, and I told them yea, then he looked down and noticed I pulled out some of the dude hair. I gave it to the cop, so I had to think why someone would come try to rob me all of a sudden, so I called my home boy that was over there, and he picked up after the 2nd time calling him. I told him what happened and told him who it was and asked him do he know where he might be and he told me so I told the cops and the cops went to go arrest him. They wanted me to point him out in court, but I said no, I wanted to be done with it, so they left me alone about it. That was one attempt but it sure wasn't the last. I was still cool with homie for a lil while longer because he used to buy drugs from me and one night he came but this time he had some x pills with him because he loved to be high and I never got high. All I did was get money, so I told him let me but two of them pills before you leave, and he did. After he left I already had this female over, so I asked her would she try it with me and she said yes. I popped off first then she did, but it hit me quicker and my body started to feel so good, I started to slide on the floor and shit and my dick got so little to it was a shame. All I could do is talk and make my money because I was up and after some time all we did was have sex all day and night. I'm making all this money and I done started using drugs but it didn't stop me from getting money or women as a matter of fact I had two other females I was sexing at the time and I wanted them to try it, so the female I already had me I told her I had to go somewhere that was to my other female house so I could let her try it and that's what I did. I took her one and from then she liked it but while I'm over to her house I have the one female in the car waiting on me, so we can go back to my place and chill but being that I done got my other chick to take one I couldn't leave her right then, so I stayed a lil while longer. When I knew she was alright then I got back in my car with the chick I already had and left and went back to my place. Now the chick I was already with we was real cool at this point, I had money everything I needed and I didn't need her for shit but her company as a matter of fact before I started taking the pills she never wanted to go home cause she stayed with her mom and I use to tell her aye you need to call your mom and let her know that you are OK but she never wanted too. I asked her why she didn't want to go back home, and she told me that her and her mom really don't get along like that, so I told her you still need to call her before she have the cops looking for you, but she didn't care. She stayed with me for a day or two and I was feeling sorry for her because of the things she was telling me about her mom and that was one of the worst things I could ever do but after a day or two together we talked and talked and she letting me know how she living and the thing was is her and her dad never really had a bound so she was missing that and her and her mom don't get along so she had me feeling sorry for her, but I told her to lets go to her house so she can get more clothes and when we walked in her room it had clothes and shit everywhere. I'm like damn this is how you live so she start packing but the freak in me wanted some of her right then so while she was packing I walked up behind her while she standing by her room door and start sexing her and after a minute or two her mom walked in and the only thing was stopping her was because I had her behind the door giving it to her so her mom couldn't push the door open all the way open on us, but that sure was a close call. After she got her things we left headed back to my place, now as I'm being friends with this female she was cool and I still had my other lil ladies on the side and she knew because when I met her I told her that I just want a friend and that I have a lady friend already, so all I wanna do is chill and if we end up taking this far the it is what it is. She was cool with it but one day my lil lady had come over I guess looking for me and this is the same female that got me the place, so she come over and I guess notice a car she never seen before out there, so what she does is fuck the car up. When I came out the door with the chick we notice her car fucked, so I told my lil female friend that have to be my other lil lady and she is going crazy and she was but that didn't stop ol' girl from fucking with me. It was times when she did want to stop fucking with me, but it wasn't because I was doing her wrong. For me I think she just never had a good man like me in her life and she didn't understand why and how she got me. It was something about her I was liking a lot and it made me want her and besides she was pretty, and I wanted to show her the good life to get her away from her hurt with her fam.

One thing I come to find out is you can never take the place of the love a kid wants from their parent and I wanted to be there for her as much as I knew how but her mom had her in this zone. Her mom knew she was liking someone so what her mom did was played like she liked her daughter and had me to come over to her house one day to meet her. I did, and I was respectful, but I could tell her mom was up to no good from being in the house with her the day I was over there, but I was cool and chilled out for a minute but the whole time I'm checking the mom out and how she is. It just seemed like she was mad, lonely, and wanted to be around her kids the whole time and being that I was taking one child away from her, she had a plan up her arm to get me away and out the pic. I didn't know how she was gonna go about doing it, so I had to wait and see. As time went on I ended up having a baby with this female and by this time I had done moved to another place. Where I was living at this point and time this new place had two lakes out there, but I stayed in the back at first, so I wasn't a problem. I stayed there for about a year then I moved to another apartment in the same area but in the front this time and one my son was watching TV with baby momma while I was in the room sleep but when I wake up my baby momma got my son in her hand soaked, so I'm like what happened to him and she tell me a lady found him in the lake drowning, so I got to find out how did he get out and I look on the porch and find a lil hole. He got out of the hole to follow the ducks and that's how he fell. The lady that found him was a white lady and she called the cops and they came to my place to ask questions and they left. The next day DCF came to my house talking about they want us to take some parenting classes, but my attitude was so bad that day and I was mad and that my son somehow got out the house anyways and at this time I'm young in the mind, so I tell them I don't need no class to take care of my son. I told them no I wasn't doing it, but baby momma was saying she would so, one of the ladies was white and the other was black but the reason why I was so mad is because it was an accident and when I was 8 they (DCF) took me from my mom. I was going off and that as one bad thing to do because two days later that same lady came knocking on my door and my son ran to the door and they heard him, so I opened the door and she had a cop with her. They came to take my son from me and that was the worst day of my life. Not just because DCF took my son but because he was going to stay with my baby momma mom and she didn't like me. I knew she would be doing the most with my son trying to turn him against me and that's what she was doing. I mean I got to visit him once a week but every time I seen him he wanted me to stop letting the people that brought him to stop taking him away from me but I couldn't do nothing to help my son but come every visit. That was getting old to the both of us, I know my lil man and he was real hurt about him not being able to go with me and I was too. One day I just stopped going because it was to hurtful for the both of us not saying it was the right thing to do at the time, but I had to do it before I did something crazy. His mom could see him, and she let us see each other but it still wasn't the same. My son had missed a lot being gone from that long of time but after some time God blessed us to be back together but now he have a lil brother and a lil sister, but we still have our bound. No matter what I just pull out pics to show him how we use to vibe and it all come to him, but I love him so much he's my heart and the reason is because he has been through so much just like his daddy coming up as a lil boy and he is so much like his daddy. I love my other two but it's something about this child that I'm just messed up about. After that situation it really made me change my attitude for the good because having a bad attitude will fuck up your life. I look back at the day when that lady came to get my son and wanna cry so bad and say to myself I wish I would have listened to them ladies and just took the parenting class and when I did take the classes it wasn't all that bad and I learned a lot from the class but now I know.

 Now I'm 32 years old, in prison haven't seen my kids, my first baby momma wanna change my first son from Jr., all the friends that was there when I had money are all gone, my best friend is gone, my baby momma don't want me no more and send me money on my books when she want too, all my brothers are in prison besides one, my mom and her boyfriend send me money through my baby momma when they have it. I mean I feel like all the real I did it made people hate me even more and I'm not saying I didn't do my share of bad, but I guess it's coming back to bit me in the ass. I have to deal with it but one thing nobody can say is T Dog didn't keep it real. I kept it so real I was blind but now I see. They thinking I'm done but I'm not and whoever is reading this book just know never worry about someone else loving you cause if you love yourself and keep God first you will never be last and loving yourself is the best love because you won't hurt yourself and always remember money don't make you real.

Tristian

AKA T Dog

I do wanna say this after all I have been through and all the trouble I been in, I really feel like I'm still here for a reason because the two times the dudes tried to come rob me I never really got hurt and those dudes did go rob somebody 1 out of them 3 dudes are in prison for 40 years and another one is still in jail because he was involved in a killing that happened in our city. I can say that I feel God spared my life because he wants to use me because those nights that them dudes came to rob me I could have got killed or shot but I didn't.

Chapter 2

Hood Life

After moving in the hood with my homeboy, I knew I needed a job, so I started working with his mom in the mall at Belk's in the back it was a pretty cool job and the people that worked there was cool too. We worked in the back-putting sensors on the clothes, so people won't steal them, and I can say that the money as pretty good too. I got payed every two weeks and my pay checks was around 4 to 500 dollars and at the time I really ain't know no better. Coming from the country to town it was a different speed just a lil bit and what I mean by that is these boys in town is really dressing, so I had to catch up on my dressing while staying in town because my homie had at least every Tommy Hilfiger shirt it was in the mall in his closet. Him and his mom had a lot of lil chains on their neck like Mr. T and the things I had was like nothing for town, so I had to rally do something about my wardrobe. Shiit, I remember my homeboy would stop by my house and go in my closet and be picking up my clothes picking at them, so when I use to get paid we would go to the mall and shop a lil bit. I would buy some Tommy and he would buy some but his would cost more because I was only buying the T-Shirts at the time and he was buying the Tommy shirts with the collar but when we stepped out we both was clean. Moving to town really made me step my game up because these boys was living the fast life. I worked with his mom for at least six months and then they laid us off. Now his mom been working there way before she got me on and as a matter of fact that's where we sometime got our Tommy from was Belks cause his mom could get is discounts when she was there.

After I got laid off I could and should have looked for another job, but I didn't. I started to sell dope, so what I did cause my homeboy was already in the streets. All I did was ask him what do I sell this piece for and this piece for and he told me, so what I did was watch the dudes that was hustling in the day time how to run to the cars but I never seen my homeboy run to no car in the hood. The dudes that was hustling out there would run to the cars or make them pull in the hole, so they wouldn't be in the middle of the road. I watched them do that and I would stay up till late to do it because you had to be on your shit to get money with them boys out there because sometime 2 and 3 niggas would run to one car at one time to make a sell. Some niggas would slap your dope out your hand just to make a sell and some would just be faster than you are and get to the car faster then you. I knew I wasn't all that ready for that so I would wait till everybody went in, then it was my turn to get money, so everybody zap that would come in the hood that wanted to buy some dope I would run to the car and tell them to meet me somewhere else, then I would serve them. I would tell them not to come back in the hood because people out here will rob you but I will bring it to your house and you don't have to drive nowhere just sit home and call me whenever you need me and I'll come wherever you want me to come. That's how I got on while my homie was in the house sleep, I was outside getting it. He was getting money too, but he had his on his phone and that's what I was trying to make it too. The only thing with my homie, he would go to sleep early and his phone would be ringing, so what I would do is pick his phone up too and get money. He didn't care, but after I got like 5 zaps on my phone and they would call me to come wherever they was I didn't have to run at no cars at night no more. I just had my first baby momma get that apartment and I would use her car to go catch them for whatever they wanted…20, 40, 60, and 100. No matter what it was I was going to see them and I treated them right no matter what, no matter how late it was I was going, and the bad thing about it I really never had any DL's. I'm not saying that was cool not to have DLs I'm saying, I just never took out the time to go back and get them and being that I didn't I got in a lot of trouble because I didn't. I have been to jail a lot because I didn't have

DL's, but the first time I even went to jail was because I was riding with my I guess so call homeboy. He got in another lane without putting on his blanker and a cop got behind us and pulled us over for it but what got me was he gives me his bomb to do whatever with and me not being hip to the game, when my homie pulled over for the cop I dropped the bomb out the window. The cop called me out the driver side and took me to jail for possession of crack cocaine. I go to jail and I didn't stay long and I wasn't scared at all to go and my homie got me out asap but I was saying to myself why would he give me his bomb and he been in the streets. I said to myself it will never happen again but I showed the nigga imam G about this shit. I'll take this one but never again because nigga you think you have a duck for a friend and at the time I couldn't see the sign because I was busy showing love, so one day we was coming out the hood and he thought a cop was getting behind us and he tried me again talking about hold this. I told his ass hell no, so he had to throw it out the window his self because I sho' wasn't going to. You got me once but not again weak ass nigga lol but he still my nigga but after I told him, no he never tried me again with that bullshit. I really start to feel like he was never my friend. He just liked the fact that I could pull women like him and I would ride for him but do you think he was the same? Hell no, a nigga like that only care about his self and me and him was friends all the way till he went to prison lol. That was for 4yrs, ever since high school and while he was out, he always said that I was going to prison because all the driving I was doing, and he could have been right. One thing I did learn from the nigga is to save your money and I was good at that, that's something I was good at even when I even young. I learned to get a lawyer, so it was nothing to me and not only that God had my back the whole time and I didn't even know it, but I did grow up in the church and never stop going just because I was in the streets. I even had my homie come to church sometime. He would tell everybody that I was going to go to prison and I never understood why he would talk like that or speak that on me like that. It's cool it wasn't no pressure because if it came down to it I would buy my way out if I could and that's what I did, but guess who go to prison first... my homie. Not only that I was very sad for him because I never wanted to see him in a place like that. No matter what and I knew how we was living, so for him to be took from the streets it hurt me, so what I did was I made sure I wrote him a lot and sent him pic's and we stayed writing each other. He had 4yrs to and I made sure I stayed in touch, but in the end it didn't even matter shiit I did everything he wanted me to do besides send him money like that, because I knew that this nigga might get out and act like he don't have to talk to nobody and everybody owe him and it's pay back when really the shit he was saying came back on him…life!

Chapter 3

Dope Game

Selling dope was never my dream and to keep it real I only did it because I was living in a drug area and the money was easy to get and to top it off my best friend at the time was already selling it.; Being that I was hangin with him it didn't make it no better. Once I got a taste of that fast money it was all over. I just kept goin and goin but for me it came kind of easy because once I got like 2 or 3 zaps the 2 or 3 people had me making enough money to not even stay in the hood. That's when I ended up getting baby momma #1 to get an apartment so I could move out from my homie momma house. Once I moved out being that I was able to drive my baby momma car anytime I got a call from one of my people (zap) I would drive but I never went and got my DL's. One day I go back to the country where I used to stay at with my grandma and my older brother end up being out there too. This one night I stopped to holla at him and he get in the car, so I tell him that I have some dope I'm trying to get off of, so he tell me that's it's money out here in the country. Being that he's my big brother and he been staying out here in the country I took his word for it. Why the fuck did, I do this with this nigga when he never sold dope in his life. All he did was hang around some of the niggas that sold it and he smoked a lot of weed that's all, so as we riding and talking he point to this truck that pass by, so me listening to big brah I get behind the truck and flash the truck down and stop the truck. I pulled up beside the truck, told the white man that I'm good, and if he need anything hit my phone. I gave him my number and you best believe he called me that same night but after

I gave him my number me and my brother looked at each other like damn that was easy and he looking at me like I told you nigga I know what I'm talking about, it's money out here. Yea its money out here all right, that white guy called me that night and I had my baby momma car but I was hanggin in the hood after I left the country from being with my brother. Dude called me later that night and I told him to meet me to this store, so he hit me with he need 40, so I tell him ok. I got to the store but I get there before him, now I'm backed in waitin on him to pull up and when he do pull up he have two women in the car with him and he tell me over the phone that the women had to go in the store to get money out of the ATM. When they pulled up next to me I looked and seen the women the women get out and go in the store. While I sat there and waited for them to come out the store but guess what they never came back out, so as I'm waitin I noticed they haven't came out yet. When I looked back at the store to see if they was coming, then I looked forward and a cop was pulling right there in front of me to block me in. He put the lights on me and pulled me out of the car… got the $40 worth of dope off the seat and checked to see if it was real and it was shiit, I even looked like a big time D boy. I had on two big chains, mine and my homeboys, so when I looked at the cop I knew him. He was a white dude I had went to school with, shiit that didn't matter either cause he still took my ass to jail for possession of cocaine. I said to myself, "My brother tried to do that shiit and I shouldn't listened to his ass, this nigga don't know shit bout the streets." That didn't stop me from selling dope I just said, "Damn, I have to be smarter next time and not listen to nobody and if they say it's a zap let them go get the money themselves and bring me back mine. G Shit! Now it was good shit about selling dope tho, shiit you get all kind of shit while you in the hood…shiit you might get some clothes one day, somebody might come through with a TV or VCR, shiit you might even meet a fine woman that might like you and wanna suck your dick for some dope. I mean you get all kind of shit for the low shiit somebody might come through and wanna sell their fuckin car or CD player out the fuckin car. Then you have the zaps that will try you and take your dope and try to run, you have zaps that come through the hood and lie and say they have money and don't, and when you give them the dope they pull off on your ass shiit your hand can even be in the window and they still gone pull off on your ass. It go down in the hood, I remember one of my zaps had me to come over to him and his lady house...now me and this zap was real cool he was like a real friend to me, so I go to his house and he buy some dope but this night him and his lady was in the freaky mode and I the one he call. So my buddy tell me he want me to fuck his girl for them and the reason he want me to do this is because my dick is bigger than his and she want it in the ass, so I'm like wow are you for real and he like yes, so while he is getting head from his lady I'm fucking her in the ass, so I'm hitting her from the back doggy style and all of a sudden as I'm stroking in and out I start to see something on the condom and this was feeling kind of good but I started to smell this shit. I stopped and tell my zap aye man I have to stop because I smell shit man, so my zap stop getting head and go get something to whip the shit up, shiit I didn't even nut that night. I left after all that shit, but I didn't stop coming by to serve them shiit they were like a friend to me, so if he asked me to do him a favor and it was something I could stand doing I would do it for him. That's how that hood shit be sometime, dope can get you all kinds of shit. A bitch will try and sell their momma fuckin house and it ain't fuckin hers...

Chapter 4

Doing Jail Time

After going to jail that one time, I stayed going. I was going to jail for all kind of shit, driving, battery, possession of cocaine. I mean it just kept going on an on…I would bound out of jail with this black bail bound dude and I would get out of jail to sign papers, so I would know when to go to court. I'm thinking he would call me and let me know ahead of time on when I need to show up for court, but he didn't. What he did do was he had these dudes that work for him that would come get you if you didn't show up for court and I would always miss court and they would come looking for me. One day I was riding in my car, my box Chevy and I'm just riding around in town feeling the city, so being that I didn't have DL's I stayed in my mirrors to see if a cop was trying to get behind me, so I kept looking and I notice this car following me, so I would turn off but everywhere I turn the car would turn, then I seen who was in the car. I always had a good amount of gas in my car at all times just in case I wanted to do something crazy. When I seen it was one of the dudes I mashed it on his ass and at the time I only had a 305 in my car, but it was fast shiit fast enough to get him off my tail, but that wasn't the last time. One time the same dude seen me in the club I use to go that was in the city and this night I had on some shorts that was starched hard, but they looked good on me and this night I'm walking around the club, so I noticed this big dude following me and looking at me crazy, so I tell my homie that I seen in the club that I think this dude is following me. All at the same time I was hooked on the red chick that was walking around in the club and I was waiting for the right time, so I could shoot her my number. Well dude had started to follow to much, so I told my homie that I was finna go. As I started to walk out the door to leave I get down the hallway and when I hit the door I started to run for the parking lot from the parking lot to the highway and when I got across the highway and hide behind a big ass tree the fucking dude was right behind me. I was fucking caught, so he brought me back to the club so the cops can take me to jail. The reason I couldn't run fast that night because of the shorts I had on…I stayed in and out of jail like it was the club but the lawyer I was getting she was the hottest in the city, so he would make the case go away. The longest I had to stay in jail was 120 days and that was before I started to get a lawyer, but I would go all the time and after a lot of niggas from my hood would go to jail and prison and not get out for a while niggas that I thought was my friend started to hate on me like damn how this nigga keep getting out, but everybody else stay in jail or go to prison. Niggas wanted to see me go down, I was staying out too long and not go to prison. One day I go get a hair cut from a dude that had been cutting my hair for the longest, so he start asking me what happened to me in this case and that case, but this day the nigga got an attitude one day talking bout damn nigga why you (me) don't stay in jail and this nigga that was older then me and we was cool as hell but that didn't stop him from hatin on li lol me. I brushed it off like it ain't shit, so I guessed he noticed that too so dude started to mess up my cut and how I noticed that was when I would get home I would look in the mirror and see where he had pushed my edge back, so I started telling him, so dude get an attitude with me and told me this your last cut and gave me back my money…pussy nigga!

Now when I would go to jail and have to sit there for some days or so I would know people and when I get in the pod where I'll be staying at I would first chill out and lay down and think on how I was going to get out. After first appearance they would give me a bound or I would have to get a lawyer to get me out faster and that's what I would do get a lawyer instead of waiting on my court date. After going to jail all them times I was saying to myself, "Man, dang my money getting low. I have kids and I just don't have money I use to have anymore for all this, so something gotta give." As long as you are selling, you are bound to fuck up sooner or later. One day I let this nigga I was real cool with hold my car and at the time I had a 99 Buick with music in it. I had 4 12's, a flip out CD Player and hives in all doors and I only let him hold my car at the time because my money had done really slowed down and he was still getting money and being that the nigga was my homie at the time and his car was raggedy as fuck I told him he could hold my car for a couple of days. After 3 days he come to my house and this night was a Friday night and the city was thick as fuck, so without me asking any questions and being that I had DL's at the time I jumped in the driver seat. So we head out where we know the city is hot at, but homie had a lot of shit in my car like a gun, pills and dope. I'm coolin thinking he gone keep it 1000, if it came down to it. If we was to get pulled over, so what I do is pull up to a store to get me some water because I had just popped an x pill, so I pay for my water while dude stayed in the car. As I'm walking out I'm drinking my water and soon as I get back to my driver door and wash my pill down good, I looked back and a car pull up behind me and at first I didn't know who it was so I say to my homie somebody done pulled up behind me. We looked back again and it was an undercover cop. I tell homie, so he could get everything and run or do something to get all them drugs off him but all he did was sit there. The cop asked me to get out the car, so I didn't have a problem with that but while I'm getting out of the car I noticed my homie still haven't made a run for it, so the cop have him get out the car too. Now the both of us are sitting on the ground while he is searching the car. First, he's on the passenger side and he find a gun under the seat, then he finds drugs in the middle piece. Now, I know and my homie know that nothing in the car is mine, so the cop go to the driver side and loom under my seat and find a lil bag with one piece of dope. He then hold it up and ask whose is this, so I say right off, "It damn sho ain't mine." The cop say, "It gotta be somebody's" on, so I say to my homie in a low voice, "aye, get right," but this nigga start to looking all sick and shit like he didn't wanna say all of it was his, like he wanted somebody to go to jail with him that night and that somebody was gonna be me. After I was telling my homie aye tell the cop that's not mine it was too late because the cop said well since nobody wanna say that it's there's all both of ya'll are going in, so I'm like fuck! I did not wanna just bust out and say it's his, so my homie end up saying its mine officer but it was too late. The cop had us in the back seat hooked and ready to be booked. As we both are in the back seat handcuffed my homie got weed on him, so he telling me to get this weed he have in his hand. I had my hands behind my back sitting in this backseat with him, calm because I just done popped this damn pill and this nigga talking in a low as talking about aye get this weed, and throw it out the window. I looked at this nigga like nigga you must be fucking crazy. I'm not doing shit else to help you and how you get the cop to let down the window, he tell the cop it's hot can he let down the window. I said to myself, how come you didn't think of a bright idea when we was just in the damn parking lot for you to lose that fucking weed, but all I tell the nigga is hell no you got that on your own homie. I'm already in the backseat with you. As we riding and we get to the jail, I'm all calm and shit, shiit I can't even be mad because I just popped off. Now we both are in the booking room and he have to tell the cop that he have weed on him and me the only thing I'm thinking about is I just got this damn $500 and now I gotta bound out of jail with it. I wasn't mad, I was happy that I had the money to be able to bound out with it, but still in the back of my head as I could think a lil bit I was saying damn this is all my fuckin money right here. I could have just sat there for a couple of days to see what would have happened being that my homie did tell the cop that all the drugs was his even tho it was too late. I could have plead not guilty and see if they would have dropped it or not, but being that I hadn't been locked up for a minute I didn't feel like sitting there for all than time. After I got out after some days or so my charges was dropped and my homie stayed in jail and ended up going to prison on all them charges. As time go on I still had a plug at this time and I was trying to get him to front me some white girl because our city was dry at the time. He had me on this wait shit, now this is the same plug I brought my first brick from and fuckin with my plug my whole grind fucked up because when I did buy a brick from him, he let me get it for $15,000. He told me that if I was to get off this one fast he would give me 50 of them. Not knowing too much about streets and niggas running game like that, I fuckin believed the nigga. after I get my first brick from him I get back to my spot and open my first brick in this big ass bowl and I'm saying to myself like damn this is a lot of fuckin coke and if I get off this one and dude gone get me 50 of them, I'm Gucci like fuck! I hit up everybody I knew that could buy what I had fast and when I was done selling the brick, I had made a $3000 profit, so me at the time was good cause I made that $3000 in one day. I hit dude up like aye I'm done I need more, so he tell me he'll hit me back and he do hit me back but the price go up to $18000, so I say fuck it OK I got it. I send that to him after he get my fucking money he kept my fucking $18000 for 4 months, so I'm going crazy about my money and at this time I'm with his sister but this nigga still haven't gave me my money back yet. I'm thinking I know this nigga ain't just try me like that so I get his sister to call the nigga and he give her this bullshit ass story about he at war with these Mexicans and shit, so now I'm start to get mad at his sister and start to put pressure on her about this nigga and I was going to hurt her if her brother was trying to buck me on my money and I didn't wanna hurt her, but I was saying in my head this nigga gonna have to feel me. After 4 months he give it back (all $18,000) and I was so happy. All I did was spend, spend, spend and while I'm spending the economy is going bad and work in the city was getting bad and I was buying everything I wanted. When my money got real low I hit him up and told him about my city was dry on coke and I needed him to front me something to get back right. Well, by this time being that I was broke I didn't really feel like that boss no more, so I'm asking him for help when really I helped him come up. Like I say he had me waiting and then one day I get a half of brick from him. When I get the brick, I'm thinking I'm finna brake this down this time, but he wanted me to sell it whole, but by the time I had found out that he wanted me to sell it whole. I had already broken it down, so when I do talk to him he mad that I broke it down, so he wanted me to just get him his money now I tell him I'll have it just chill. I was thinking about bucking the nigga but I knew he had people out there to be able to do something to me and I was still fucking with his sister strong. I was playing it smart as I knew, so what I did was tried to cook some of the coke and after that I see why he was mad that I broke it down. The coke was not all that good like my first brick I brought from him. Now I gotta work with this bad coke, so what I do is hit one of my other homies up and meet up with him, so we can do some business. My homie trade me some pills for some of the coke I had. Now I got pills and coke so one night I get a call from this female that want some pills, so I tell her to meet me at this store and me not thinking I leave to meet her, but this night I have my gun in the car and the reason I had my gun on because I always said after those dudes tried to rob me that one night at my old place that I would always leave the house with my gun if it's at night and that's what I did. I go to meet her and I get to a stop sign and don't make a complete stop and a cop get behind me. I put the gun and drugs in this hiding spot I had in my car then the cop pulls me over and all I could think was I was just in the same situation with my other homie, so I try and blink my eyes to see if I was dreaming. Come to find out I wasn't, the shit was real I was being pulled over with a gun and drugs in the car. Now I'm out on bound and I'm doing good with not getting in trouble and after two years I get into with baby momma #2 but let me tell you how these lawyers work. I would go see my lawyer I been getting for a minute the only lawyer I have ever had. I would stop by to drop off money or see what the state had on me about the situation and my lawyer wouldn't have nothing and all she would tell me is she is going to continue my court date. With me not knowing too much about the court system, I'm just happy and be like OK I'll see you in court on whatever date she gives me. One day I stopped by to give my lawyer my portfolio of pics to her and she just look at my pics like yea whatever, so I leave but I'm thinking she would put it in my file to see if that could help if needed and the reason I even had a portfolio was because after I got pulled over that night I decided to try something else with my life and that was modeling. I never had a dream, I never wanted to even be a model. All I knew was I wanted to stop getting in trouble and stop giving this lawyer all my fucking money like I been doing and over the time while I was selling dope people would always tell me I was cute or I should model my hair, so I said to myself fuck it, I always go to the club and take pics, so why not try modeling shit, I got swag. I went to the place in my city that was doing modeling and acting and I asked them what do I need to do to start and they told me everything I needed to do to get started and that was call this photographer, so I could set up a photoshoot. I did it and it was a lady who I shoot with. We did the shot, it was at a park and she was nice. She told me a lil on what to do as for posing and I did it. After we was done she told me that she would call me when she was done with my pics, so she could give me my pics on a CD. I told her OK thanks. I got the CD back and I looked at the pics and I'm like damn these pic's look real nice, so I put them on the website called ExploreTalent.com and another website call Modelmayhem.com and before I knew it photographers was messaging me like crazy for shots. I was like dang this is crazy lol, so I did like four other shoots before I made this comp card to give my lawyer and like I said she looked at it like it was nothing, like I'm not supposed to be doing anything but selling dope and paying her to get me out of jail or do a lil time. I had other plans with my life, so I come back to her this last time and she hit me with dang man you haven't gotten in trouble yet. No baby momma drama or nothing and I'm like no, but in my head, I'm like this lady is not for me, but I play it cool so after I left that day I was living with baby momma #2. After 2 years of doing good out on bound me and my baby momma get into it over something small and the cops get called and I went to jail. Now they won't let me bound out because I wasn't supposed to get in trouble while I was out from the gun charge, so now I have to sit. I'm not wanting to sit, but I had to, while I'm sitting in there, there was some things I was learning and after 75 days of being in jail I get out on 2 years probation which was a good deal for me even tho my charges was supposed to get dropped because they didn't have shit on me. What my lawyer did was while I was in court on the 75th day she came to me and said that the state will offer you 2 year probation right now or we can wait for another week and take this trail, so I'm thinking like damn I wanna go home and I'm thinking I don't wanna go to trial while I'm sitting in jail and not only that my lawyer not even acting like she wanna even try to fight for me, so that day I left with 2 year probation. I get out on probation, go back in after doing everything for my probation after doing 14 months of my probation for VOP. Now this time I sit for 23 days after getting another lawyer that I didn't know, but he ended up being cool and had the same name as mine. He got me back in court on reinstate, but this time the judge put me on house arrest for 1 year and regular probation for a year, so that is 2 years all together. Yes, I fucked up and my luck is really running out on me, but after being out on house arrest I stayed out for 2 months and VOP again. When the cops came to my house it's like 11:00 at night and I was just about to lay down that's when my kids came to me and said, "Dad, there's someone at the door." I'm thinking it's my next door neighbor, so I just open the door and the cops was standing right there to get me. One cop was black and he knew who I was because we go to the same gym and the other cop was a white man with a dog. The white cop with the dog walked away and another white cop and the black cop came in, so I could get all my white's that I needed and they let me hug and kiss all my kids before I left. This time you already know what they finna do to me, send my ass to prison and that's what they did. 2 years and 24months I have to spend in prison away from my family and kids. I guess my luck really ran out because this time I didn't have the money to get a lawyer. I really had to go to prison and that's where I'm at writing this book.

 The bus came to get us from the jail around 4:00 am and it's about 15 of us that's going on this trip and 2 of the dudes I knew because they were from the same city I'm from. We're all on the bus headed to the prison on the interstate and I'm thinking in my head like what the hell is this finna be like, boi I hope it ain't like what I see on TV damn, so what I do is think out loud and ask one of the dudes that's on the bus with me and they give me the whole run down on how its going to be and what to do. I'm listening to them the whole time, but I'm thinking to myself fuck that I have to see for myself because these dudes might be a lil different from me when it comes down to this. They talking about follow them and I'm like OK, but in my head I'm thinking these niggas might be up to something. I don't know what it is and I'm not finna find out. Now we are pulling up to the prison and we get here early and have to sit there for a hour or so before they let us in, so all the inmates are sitting and talking about who all locked up and how much time they got or getting. I mean it just goes on and one, then after that hour the officer start the bus, so he could drive us in the gate and once he did that it was time to do time. We get off the bus and walk in the back and once all the inmates are in the back they close the door and all you see is other inmates from other counties and all of the inmates that got off our bus. I was looking at about 50 males and about 10 different officers and the first thing they tell us to do is take everything off and put everything in this black bag they was passing around (that's what we did), so now all of us are naked with our hands down by our side nothing but nuts and balls. We all in line up and walk through the metal detector. Once all of us are through, we all are sitting there just listening on what to do. The officer want to see our hands, our feet, in our mouth, behind our ears, under our nuts. Then the part that I really hated the most was when he told us turn around face the wall and put our head on the bench. Our ass in the air and spread our ass so he can look and see if we had anything in there, now me being me I didn't stay bent over like that because I wasn't with that shit, but I did it tho. Then they was telling us how to answer the officers with yes sir, no sir and yes ma'am/ We had to yell that out so it would be stuck in our head and when we got there I still had my long dreads, so the officers hurried up and put me in the chair to get a cut, so off with the dreads all the way bold. I really didn't wanna look in the mirror, but when I passed by the mirror I looked like a fuckin skin back bird lol. I was moving fast but I was able to see myself and I'm thinking in my head like oh shit I look fucked up on the outside but on the inside I was still T Dog. I didn't let anything break me all I did was stay away from mirrors until my hair grew back. There was one thing I did think about and that was if I was going bold and how I would look if I have to play a bold head when I get out. I had to get my mind right for that part, but as time went on all I did was pray and ask God to be with me and please never leave me, so all my worries went away at the time. I was never the type of dude that stayed looking in the mirror anyways. I came to realize that if you have a good heart and work out you will shin like a light and for one God will shin through you so bright that when people look at you all they will see is nothing but God in you. That is real beauty when a person see the love of God in you. I'm not saying you don't wanna look good on the outside of your body, but when you come to a place like prison it is designed to break you down and rebuild you into a better person, don't let it break your mind down and you not wanna get back up you got to be strong and try your best to say Lord I need help and keep calling on him because he will keep you strong. Yes, I know you might have family and kids out there, even a girlfriend. If they with you while you're doing your time then that's a blessing and if they start to rid with you and then stop it's gonna hurt but just remember to call on God and ask him for help and to be with you and keep you strong while you do your time, but while you are in prison don't just lay down and let the time do you. If you're going to lay down, lay down and think of something you good at. Like me I felt like I never and the only talent I did have was the women loved the shit out of me. I never knew I was handsome, no one ever really told me that while I was coming up. I just knew the girls just use to like me like shit and how my attitude was everybody thought that I knew I looked good, but it wasn't that I just had a bad attitude from coming up. Not because I knew I looked good, until over the years everybody just kept saying he cute or he so handsome and when I use to go see my real mom they would be like Betty, he so cute or handsome, so in my head I started to think like it must be true about me being handsome. Every time I would take a pic all of them would come out real nice, so after I got in trouble the last time for the gun I started to do the modeling, because I stayed taking pics and the reason why I stayed taking pics of me was because of memories. Some people think I did it for other reasons but that's not the case. I did it because I was away from my real mom for her to take pics of me and every foster home I was to we never really took pics, so I would get my brother to take pics of me and when I got older and started going to the club, we would always take pics of that night we went out, so what I'm telling you is it might be on the dark side for you right now but let me tell you never let your mind give up on you because a mind in a sad thing to waste. You are good at something you just have to think of what it is, and sometime God put people here in prison, so they can try to come up with something to do then be out there selling drugs all your life. Never give up and love yourself no matter who don't love you. When we walk with God we leave behind a sweet fragrance that can inspire others to follow. There is something I do miss and think about a lot is all my kids. I have 4, I have 3 boys and 1 girl. My boys are 12, 6 and 4, my lil girl is 2. While I'm doing my time, this is the only thing that bother me a lil bit is I know my kids miss me a lot, it's like I can feel it in my heart and feel their heart and know that they fuckin miss me, but the bad thing about it is the 2 baby mommas I do have don't want me to really be apart of their life. My first baby momma never let me see my oldest son and she has changed his name from my last name to her last name and yes, I let her do it because I am tired of fighting with her. My second baby momma who I was living with is keeping me away from my kids in a way too even tho she writes me and let them write me and she sent me one pic each of all them to me. It's still not enough all she wanna do is write me and tell me she doesn't want me no more and she want some one better then me, someone who will never call her names, someone that will caress her body and treat her right. She moved my things out of her apartment while in prison and put them in storage because she is moving into a new place at the end of the month. That's when she will get a phone, so I can call to talk to them. Now just know this whole time she has already been approved to be able to come see me, but she hasn't made it up here yet. She writes me still like 2 times a week to tell me my kids talk about me all the time and my 4-year-old is being bad because he misses his daddy. I'm shaking my head like if you know what's wrong with your kids then why not fix it. You can write me and tell me this and that but what really matters to me is how my kids is hurting. You can have any man you want out there but at least bring my lil ones to see their daddy. I'm only an hour away from my kids and she haven't made it up here yet, haven't told me why she haven't came yet either, but imma keep it G because I have no time for stressing, all imma do is pray for my kids and ask God to please keep them safe and healthy and to keep me in their little heart. I fuckin love my kids but I been going through it about my kids so much it makes me feel like I wish I never even had kids because I can never enjoy them at all and not because me it's because I'm the good guy and I care. If I didn't care that would give my baby mommas something to talk about, but I leave no room for them to talk bad about me, so what they have to do is lie on me saying I'm in and out their life or it's my fault that I came to prison lol but one day imma say fuck the world and just keep moving the fuck on and let these so call moms go get their kids the dads they want to have in their kids life. I'm tired of fighting for my kids it's too much for one nigga to deal with. I rather wait till they get older and find me on their own.

Chapter 5

Thinking in Prison

3.21.14

In prison just coming back from work. After work I hit the track with this nigga that's from the same city I'm from, so he ask me have I ever heard him rap before and I tell him no, so he pull me to the side and spit some real shit for a nigga and it was only into of his mixtape, but dude went so hard on the intro, I'm like damn my nigga I can feel you all the way on that intro, so we take a walk around the track and chop it up and he let me in on his life and it touched me because we have been through the same thing and the whole time we was saying how do all the real niggas always end up with the fuck niggas that don't have the same love we have for them they don't have for us; I just don't understand. All the real nigga always end up with the fuck niggas who envy us in the back of their mind, then the real niggas hearts be cold because of the shit we been through and don't wanna let another nigga in…life is crazy!

On **3.30.14** I'm sitting on one of the dudes bunks talking to him and for some reason a white guy came walking by and we caught eye contact and I kept looking at him and he kept looking at me, but he was smiling a lil bit and I wasn't and after he seen the look on my face, the look on his face changed, so we kinda had words and it got a lil intent, so I stayed sitting and he kept walking and after I left the dude bunk were I was sitting and I went to my bunk and started reading the book I been reading which is Michael Vick Autobiography. As I'm reading I'm saying to myself like damn I feel kind of bad by the way I acted toward dude and it just kept eating at me, so after head count I went over and told him I was sorry for the way I acted earlier and he said it takes a real man to do what I did and we shook hands and did a lil hug and talked a lil bit and it made me feel so good about the way I came at him when I know I was wrong. He told me that he was really just speaking not trying to start something and I just said my bad brah that's not even me anymore to be a bad ass, I leave that to the young kids. I'm 32 years old and I'm trying to better myself and we both smiled and walked out for chow!

I guess Michael Vick book is inspirational after all…just one of them days in the chain gain the devil tried to use me but God was not having it because it was eatin me up on the inside. I love the new guy I'm becoming not that I was that bad before I got here in prison but by being in here you just wanna try to be better so when you get out people can see that you're a better person. You have to try not let the devil use you and get you in trouble or wanna fuss and fight. I have kids and I wanna show them how to be funny and make people laugh and only fight when you have too. I mean don't be a push over but stay smiling if you can and when you start to get down get off to yourself or go talk to someone if you have that someone to talk to. I'm not saying I can't and won't get mad, but I can say this, I'm trying to be more and more positive and with that you get a positive outcome. One thing I can say about my time here in prison is that the ladies here that see me don't mind telling me how beautiful my smile is and being that I'm doing the modeling still when I get out it let me know that I still have a look that people will notice if I get around the right people. To tell the truth I can't model I just been told that I'm handsome, cute and have a nice smile that is what have me doing the modeling and so far, I'm still learning about modeling and acting, but one thing about it all, I really feel like I have what it takes to become a great model and anything I learn I get better and better…I do everything to perfection! I also do this for the kids out there that might be in a foster home or a home they don't wanna be at, but I just want yall kids to know is don't give up, be strong, read books, don't be bad in school, try your best to learn everything about yourself and in school, pray, talk to someone that will listen to you and not judge you or what you're going through and after you try these things I bet one of them will work for you if not all of them. I know it's going to be hard sometimes but think, nothing in this world is easy not even getting a boyfriend or girlfriend is easy it's all hard, but when you work hard in the end it's all worth it…just remember when we fall down then we get up, then we go harder than ever before because we know way more then we did before, so try your best to be smarter and be a leader…plain out just have confidence! About anything you do and that will take you a very long way…even if you can't do it act like you can and just try hard and wait to see the outcome…it will be so funny to you. Don't get mad just do you and be good at being you.

Thinking in Prison

4.16.14

I had a dream last night about some of the things I use to do or was doing while I was in the streets hustling. I woke up to read my Daily Bread for today and it reads about a young man being adopted by Christ Jesus and that's how I feel like even tho I was placed in different foster home in my life time and it all was a part of God's plan for my life. Even tho He knew what He was doing, I didn't have a clue at all. All I did was just rolled with what was going on at the time. Now as I'm rolling I really never payed any attention to where I was really going. The only thing I was able to notice was sometimes my roll was slow and a lot of times it was fast, but now that I have a lot of time to sit here and think about a lot of my life I can really say God really love me because with all the stuff I have done in the streets as far as selling dope or someone trying to rob me, I'm still here and not dead, I'm like wow!, He really love me I mean yes I'm in prison, yes I have baby momma bullshit, yes my friends are all gone, yes I was in foster homes but I still hold my head up and say yes Jesus loves me a lot and people say dang dude you strong and all I can say is God made me like this… now out of the things I have done in the streets if Jesus was not by my side I would have been in the FEDS or dead, but Jesus have really been there for me and I'm so thankful to say he's been there. That's why I feel so blessed and hardly stressed because God is great! A lot of times when I say I be by myself I really don't, I be with God the whole time talking to him trying to get closer to him by trying to understand what it is he want me to be doing with my lil life. I can say I am trying different things with my life that's positive, to see where imma land and hoping I land somewhere that will make me truly happy for me and my kids, because that's one of the main things I feel like I have problems with is my kids. Having a bond with them like a father should because I know kids need their dads and I never had my dad there for me like I wanted, so I wanna give that to my own kids. Only if I can and what I mean by that is if there moms ain't with the bull then imma be there because the way I feel none of my kids came here by mistake they all got here because I wanted to have them, so I'm not finna fight with my kids moms just to be in their life because to me that's too much stress for my child and me, so what I do is ask God to please be there for my kids like you was and have been there for me and I truly feel like God will and when they get older to make their own moves then if they still have care in their heart, then they coming to find me and then we will finish what we started. One thing I can say is I was there when all my kids was born and when I was still with their moms. I go hard with playing with them and taking care of them and taking pics, so they can look back and say my dad was there. I mean my mom used drugs and me and my brothers was taken from her while in school and as I got older I would get anybody I knew at the time to take me to her. I didn't care who it was I went to find my lady. It took time for us to really get to know each other, but I never stopped trying and now that I do know her, I love her like I never left a day in my life. I mean we act just alike lol and I love it. I think she is so cool, hood, so real and that's all me all the way and that's what make me love her so much. I mean we do have our up and downs, but I still love her! We come from the bottom and we are headed to the top to live a bigger and better life. God bless whoever is reading this and stay strong no matter how hard it get!

Thinking in Prison

4.17.14

One thing I did find out while in prison is that if you act like you don't want to jack your dick at night you better believe it will find a time to put you in the right dream to get that nut out of you. For me it like to change up on me, like I use to have wet dreams at night when I'm sleep and I hate having a wet dream, but when you be backed up so much from not having sex and you do have a wet dream your dick shoot a lot of com out and if you don't have nothing beside you to wipe it up with then your ass is just wet up. What I would do is keep my old sock that I wore for that day at night right beside my head or down by my feet at the end of my bed, so if I did have a wet dream I can grab my sock right beside me or get up and reach down by my feet to get my sock to wipe my dick if I I have one. Me trying to be strong minded and saying I'm not going to jack my dick and my baby momma would write me and tell me to just pray about it and try to keep your mind off it. I'll do all that plus more, I even would lay on my side so it wouldn't be like I was lying flat down on no one at night. It stopped for a lil while at night, but I guess after working out so much and still not jacking my dick, that shit just kept building up inside me, so what my dick and mind would do is wait til I go back to sleep after we eat breakfast in the am like 5:00 am in the morning because at night I really don't sleep that good, but in the morning after chow before I have to go to work I take a lil cat nap and the cat nap put me there. In the room with her and it be feeling so real sometimes and I be knowing deep in my mind that it's not real but in my dream my dick be in that pussy and I be trying to get that nut and I be telling her to hurry up before someone come and when I do that boom! My dick be hard as hell. I be lying on my back with my knees up pointing in the air and my dick hard right between my legs. What I do is reach for my sock real lite, so my dick won't let know nut come out. The reason for me doing that is because if I let that nut come out it's going to be a lot, so I move real lite and put that sock on my dick and pull and pull til it all come out.

Then I just lay there and think like boy when I get out she gone get it because I have a lot of pressure built up. I need some pussy bad and I refuse to jack my dick 2 and 3 times in the morning because whoever I give this good dick to she gone love the shit out of me! Should I jack my dick or wait and give it to a lil lady that's gonna love the shit out of me. I really don't know yet, but one thing I do know is I want her to be special and I want to like her. I'm too old to be just giving my good lovin away to just any female that I can just to get my rocks off even tho it can go like that but imma try to stay strong and wait it out and wait for the right female, so we can keep doing our 1-2 and not just a sex session. I want it to be more than sex. I might be out of my mind or I might be getting older and I want more out of life. I wanna be the best man she ever laid eyes on and I want her to be the sexiest, prettiest lil lady I have even laid eyes on. When I leave prison imam be more on point and my mind is going to be way mature than ever before, so to the ladies beware cause T Dog is coming!

Thinking in Prison

4.18.14

To the readers of this autobiography about me, a lot of yall may be saying "He didn't go through to much," or maybe some are saying, "He lying about these things he put in this book." What I'm doing is letting you guys know what I have been through, seen and still going through and right now I'm in prison. I don't look at it as a bad thing, I look at it as I know our God is doing all of this because this is His plan for my lie. Not only that he is putting me to the test also, but imma keep going and giving Him praise, because I won't give up. Sometimes I want too and when I start to feel like that I just start talking to God and He gives me new strength. All I can do is smile and keep going, but I have to write about my life, troubles and things I been through. To me it gets hard, real hard for me, but I just say, "Lord you know best." I have to sit and wait on Him and be on His time. The thing about His time is that his time is so perfect. When I think about that I sit back and say, "Lord, I know I will get through whatever it is I feel like I'm going through and you will make everything better, this is just a phase I'm going through to make me open my eyes and know that you are real." You are there for me in the good and bad times and I will praise when there is good and bad times. I've seen a lot, I been through a lot and I'm going to go through more, but all at the same time it make me stronger and better to see how God gets me through is what makes me worship His name. It's just my testimony and I hope it touch who ever might read this. God Bless! I really feel like God put me in prison to rebuild me for the better and when I think about it I still smile, because when I was out on the streets I started a lot of things I never did in life, like smoking and popping pills. I feel like I started to thug real hard and all at the same time I wanted a new life as far as mode/actor and if I'm going to be doing these things I need a good head on me at all times. I feel like God put me here to help me and to get my mind right, even though it's prison; He knows best. I do feel Him and I'm glad He did it. Now I can get out and start with a new start…He's rebuilding me!

Thinking in Prison

4-21-14

Just one of them dayz I'm feeling a lil down. I have not heard anything from no one as far as my baby momma and the kids or my mom. It kind of make me feel kind of alone and I can't say that I'm stress because I really feel like I'm not stressing just feel alone with no one to talk to. All I can say is, "Lord I love you and thank you for everything you have done for me." Then I pray for my kids and ask God to save me and my baby momma relationship because deep down in my heart I love her a lot and would hate to have to move on to someone else. I'm not afraid of moving on I just have been with my baby momma for so long til all I want is her and to live with my kids, so they can see their daddy and mom with each other every day as they get older. I don't know if that's going to work out like that but, I'll try my best to stay in the pic. She wrote me a letter saying that she only wanted to be friends with me and I have no problem with that. I think she wanna go out to see if she can find someone better than me but, like I told her and she already told me, I'm the best and now you looking for someone better. Ain't no dude better than T Dog if you ask me, I am the best and I know I gave her the best when we was together and I went hard enough to see if she would tell me that and she did. Imma stick with it till I leave this bitch! Now I know I can be rude and mean at times but, my good out weight my bad and that's real. When I get out of prison, what imma do is give her space and if it's meant to be then she'll come back. If she ever tell me that while I was in prison her and someone else had sex and she let another nigga put his hands on her in any kind of way imma let it be and really let her move on. The way I see it is once the pussy is mine in order for us to realy move on then all she have to do is say she had sex with someone and I'm out the pic, until then she will always have me. Not that I'm being controlling or anything I just can't stand to imagine someone else touching her and then I'm suppose to get out and be with her like it never happened. Shiit, got me fucked all the way up…I got principles that's what I live by. I don't play no fucking games. If you fuck that nigga then that nigga can have you, but that don't mean I won't fuck her no more. I just won't be with her ass like that and I know for sure she will be back soon or later and imma wait on her to come back because she have been with me so long til it ain't gone feel all the way right to be with another dude. All they gone do is fuck to see if both of them gone like it and after she is done she gone sit there and try not to think about me, but imma be tight there in the pic because we gone still be friends and not only that we have kids together. Imma be on the look out for a more badder gangsta bitch that's going to be crazy about T Dog I know I got it like that, I just have to find the right lil lady that's going to please me in every way possible and she gone be on her shit really getting to the money and pushing me if need be. I can say I'm on my shit right now shiiit, now that I'm here in prison I'm thinking of everyway I can get money besides the streets and once I can make that happen and stay out of jail or prison I'm good. Shiit, I'll be better off making money the right way that way I can move freely because the longer you stay out the more you can have...boss shit! If my plan work I'm in there if it don't I won't stop trying.

4.22.14

Thinking in Prison: Dreamin'

7:30 a.m. I meet this very pretty girl at this church gathering, she was nice, red, tall and slim with a pretty smile... so I'm checking her out and she see me looking at her so, I see her stand up and get ready to head out the door, I guess to leave or go to the back of the church (maybe to the bathroom idk). I followed her to where she might be going and I stopped her and asked her, her name. She smiled and told me her name, so I get to rappin with her for a minute or two. I asked her, "Do she have a man." I didn't see her seating next to no one. She told me no but she have a friend and she is pregnant. I looked at her belly like dang, you havin a baby in there. She smiled and said yes. Then I asked her, "How many months are you?" Because she didn't have a baby pug, her belly was flat as hell. Now for some reason I'm thinking in my head "I wonder if this girl really having a baby or is she just telling me that, to see if ima still try to talk to her." So, I keep talking to her because she seems very nice and I'm loving her smile too. She's only some weeks. That's when I said to myself, "I can make her get an abortion...I keep talking, then I asked her, "Who all have you had sex with around my city?" and she starts naming but, the first name she say is a young dude I got into it with sometime back. So, I'm like dang you use to like him and have sex with him. She kept it real and told me yeah and that dude was a very cool dude, that's why she let him get some pussy. So, I'm like dang in my head and saying to myself, "This girl must be a big hoer out this world if she let that nigga fuck. I hit her with well, let's take a walk and talk. She agreed, then I hit her with aye lil lady, a nigga feelin you and ima keep it 1000, I wanna sex you like right now! So, she was like wow! Just like that, ok then. I'm saying in my head, like I know this pussy have a bad smell. As we walking in the hood I see some homies I knew, so I go up and asked them,

"If one of them have a rubber." This one older dude I know was like "Yea homie, I got you." He gives me a rubber but, he put the rubber in between some newspaper and gives it to me. Then I tell him thanks and walk back over to the girl. Now as we walking I tell her to walk up a lil further to see if she see a car beside a red box Chevy, she tells me yea. I see with a lil girl and three kids in the car, then I told her lets go around the back. She walked straight up to this ac unit and bent over and I'm like damn she is really ready. I put the rubber on and pushed my dick right up in that pussy. It was a nice hole but, in my head I'm like this can't be real but I'm still taking my strokes. I only stoked 3 or 4 times before I wanted to nut. I'm like damn this pussy wet and it don't have a smell. Still in my head I'm like this can't be real and just before I was about to nut I woke up; It was all a dream.

Later that day…I can't see them coming down my eyes so I gotta make this pen cry. I can't see them coming down my eyes so I gotta make this pen cry! This first baby momma of mine took me to court so she could change our son name, because she no longer want me to be his dad…I don't know why she feels like this, but I can say she make me wanna hate her ass. That's not what ima do, ima ask God to fix this shit and keep moving on. I can say that it do hurt to see her wanna change lil man name for whatever reason she have. I mean, we are over and done. She have been keeping me from my son most of his life just to hurt T Dog "Me". She added to his middle name and the judge asked her, "Why would she want to change your child name." I just don't understand, so now my son T Dog Jr. is no longer mine. I no longer have any rights to him and it's sad, but I know I had to give them up because me and her can't vibe. It's not because of me, it's because of her. I wanted to be there for my son and when I was with her, I was there for him (That shit is no good because she still took him). I can say that I did let her because I agreed to give up my rights; for one: she will not let me see him, only on her time; for two: she put me on child support for no reason just to be mean and still kept him away from me. I was like, "Damn, I might as well go ahead and let her have this and I did want to get off child support." If I didn't give my rights up she still would have made it hard for me, so now it's all the way done with me and her. It's still in God's hands and not only that he is still my son, because I was the one in the room making him (humpin). I was the one to change him, keep him from crying and I was there to buy him clothes and shoes. What do I get in the end (straight bullshit)? I'm the one that wanted to be there for my son, but now it's all on them until he gets older. I did get to write him a letter and my lawyer was able to read it him in court. This was what it read: Hello T Dog Jr, I just want you to know no matter how far you go or where you might be please know that your real Dad (that's me) will always love you, I love you more than life it self, you can call me anytime you please and when you turn 18 you can even change your name back to T Dog Jr. Daddy love you! God Bless you forever!

    The good guys seem like they always get the bad end of the stick and IDK why, but I do know that if God suffered we gone have to suffer to, so here is mine. To me this shit is real bad and I really don't know how to feel. I mean I know I'm still his real Dad in real life, but this shit have me feeling some type of way (Fuck)!!!!! Lord, you need to fix this shit for real because if it ain't one thing it's some more shit and I'm not thinking about killing myself, because that's some weak shit. I can say all this shit I'm going through is really fuckin with me for real. These bitches is making me mad and I'm getting tired of all this shit. You have to be an evil bitch to want to change your son name at the age of 12 and I know my son didn't really want to do it. The only reason why he did do it, is because all the people he is staying with is and was making him feel left out. So, just to make them happy he went ahead and did it, but deep in his lil heart I know he is crying. I came back to my mom and I hope and pray he home back to me and I don't ever want to see her in life (baby momma #1). I know I love kids, but it makes me not ever want to ever have kids again in life. It's not that I didn't play it cool before I gave these females these kids. I even asked them and not only that my first baby momma, I took care of her first son before I asked her, "Will she have my son." I did that so she could see that I was and I am a good Dad to my kids, but that bitch still pulled bullshit…I still may have more kids fuck it!

Prison Time

4.30.14

    Sitting in prison thinking… I try to be so calm about a lot of things while being in here, like when talking to niggas I meet or niggas from around my way that might be stressing or have a lot on their mind and need someone to talk to, someone that will listen to what they have going on in their life and not judging them at all. Someone to be open minded about all they have to say. There is one thing I notice about that is that I can never really talk about the things I might have going on in my life, because I'm always listening to their problems. To keep it real, I don't mind listening but in some way for me it's just to help time pass. All at the same time they do have to pay because the game is to be sold and not told. I can say it do get tiring because in some way I be wanting me somebody to talk to about what I'm thinking about and someone to give me good advice about my situation or problems. I have this one dude I be kicking it with while I'm here and this nigga be having a lot of shit going on. He stay stressing about shit that he can't do shit about. I don't mind being there for him but it's like this nigga be stressing to damn much for me and the shit is starting to fuck with me at, so what I do is when he start talking about the bullshit I kind of like tell him shhit we all have something going on out there that be bothering us and I guess he can see that now I'm tired of hearing about the bullshit. So this fuck nigga start being quite, I'm looking at this nigga in the corner of me eye thinking like look at this fuck nigga. All he wanna do is stress about bullshit and since I want talk about it I guess he don't have nothing else to talk about, so you know what I say to myself, "Fuck ya, homeboy," because T Dog aint on that type of time, shhit lets talk about how we can link and get money or something. I damn sho don't wanna or gunna talk about that stress shit…to me you don't get nothing out of stressing the only thing you get out of that is ya ass gone be stuck not knowing what to do. That's not what I'm about, I'm about thinking of a plan that can make me a whole lot of money when I get out of here. How I need to be there for my kids and show them that their Dad came a long way to get where he's at, not only that I want them to look at me like I'm the best, the best Dad, the best at everything…I mean they love a lot and they also feel like Dad is the best so far. I want to show them a lot more so as they are growing up they can say, "I wanna be like my daddy." Little do they know I'm going to make them better than me…if its God will. I look back at my life and see a lot of time I played with and to keep it real I will not change it for nothing in the world. Like I say, "It made me who I am today a fukin 'G' and I won't stop till I get a mill."

5.6.14

Thinking to myself…it was all a plan for me to be in the streets selling drugs, making a lot of money and in the end having to come to prison. The reason I say that is, it's a lot more I know now that I'm here…being in prison helps you think on your life and how you can better yourself in whatever it is you wanna do. For me, I wanna better myself and God knew by letting me see all I have seen and been thru, I would want to. After my roller coaster ride it's like now I see the bigger picture and the good thing about it, God made it where it's not too late for me to have a dream. I have a dream to be the best father, son, brother, and role model ever can be. I also want to go back to school, get a job, and keep doing my modeling/acting and one day soon I'll be getting paid out the azz, so I can take care of my family how want without having to go to jail or prison again.

5.7.14

Today is a blessed day! Everyday is a blessed day just some days are better than others. What I want to talk about today is how people don't want to believe that God sent His only son to die for our sin…I'm in prison with a lot of dudes and you never really know what they be thinking, what they been through or what religion they study until you talk to them about what you believe in. For me I believe in God and I love Him so much. Whenever someone wants to talk about what they believe in and it's not Jesus, I don't run I sit there and asked them why and they tell me. My bunky don't believe that God sent His only son to die for our sins…and as we are talking he can see that I love God a lot because of how I talk. Today we started talking and we was talking about his religion and I was telling him about God and why don't he believe God sent His son. He started telling me about him reading these books and that the Bible he just don't read, but he do believe in God. My thing is if you believe in God, why you don't believe in His word, so he hit me with so many people wrote the Bible so it's hard for him to believe. When I look on his bed he had a Bible on his bed ☺ crazy! I was talking to him before about God and how I have been to jail 49 times and I'm 32 years old and I had never been to prison. He tells me that's because the choices I made, but I told him no It's not because of my choices it's because God seen the crazy things I was doing and He wanted to have my back. It really showed me that He is real; He will be there for me and have my back no matter how much trouble I'm in. He already know I have a good heart, so you know what He did for me He saved me…even though I ended here in prison He saved me. He knew by doing that I would forever give Him glory and tell others about what He has done for me, and he will do the same for you; if you get to know Him. One thing I noticed is that it's a lot of evil people, it's a lot of people that don't believe, it's a lot of people that think that they do things for themselves, but I'm here to tell you that God is real! He is a real good father, mom, friend, whatever you want Him to be just know that He is good and He move on His time not on our time. The good thing about His time, it's perfect! All you have to do is wait on Him. That's it, I'm telling you He will make you smile so big…I'm in prison and still being Blessed no matter where they put me God be right there to make me feel good and happy no matter what. It do be days where I feel alone, but I pray and it be something that He'll do that will make me smile. To all ya'll that don't want to believe I'm telling you He is real, all you have to do is talk to Him at night or just to yourself (wherever you may be). Ask Him whatever it is that you want and you will see how He works. My bunky have not been back to talk to me yet lol. I think I have him thinking, that's all. I'm not weak minded at all, when it comes to God because I know what He has done for me and some of the people I'm around, like my kids and I can tell you that He good (it's not me it's Him). A lot of people have told me that don't see me, they see the God in me and it makes me feel so good to hear that, that's how I know God is dealing with me and to tell my story to the world and reach out to the kids because the kids love me and I love them. The more people see God in me, the more a lot of people will hate on me, but I don't care because God have my back!

5.8.14

Thinking in Prison

Reading my daily bread and it was taking about a major lead baseball player named, Tony Graffanino. Each year his organization holds a week long baseball camp; during the camp they also offer a daily Bible study…the leader tried to find ways to convince the campers that God exist so they would place their faith in Him. After 13 years they had seen only three people who decided to follow Jesus, so they changed their approach. Instead of trying to present facts or winning arguments for a debate, they simply talked about the amazing life and teaching of Jesus. As a result, more campers came to listen and more chose to follow Jesus. Now I say that to tell you this, I notice when I was talking to my bunky and I be talking about how much I love God and how much he saved me from what was going on around me, he listened but all at the same he kept his distance but this gay ass nigga made sure he kept me in his view. I don't know why but when he tell me about his religion I listen and hear him out but he never give me a good reason why he don't believe God sent His only son to die for our sins. Not only that he never tell me anything good about the religion he studied, like how I can tell how many times God has saved me and out all the things I've been through and seen I'm still here. This is my first time to prison after being booked in jail 49 times…you tell me, "If good is good?" The ways things are looking to me He is amazing and I won't complain! One thing I noticed is the more you follow God or people see God in you the more they stay away or dislike you…that's what I'm experiencing! Unless, they have a good heart and they are not on that hating and see God the way I see Him they will try their best to stay away from evil/hating, they try to love people as much as they can. Some people it's hard to truly others like that because I think if they heart ain't all the way true then they will fall into the bull. If you are glad God make you and He have saved from whatever then you're better off. Hating on the next man/woman will not get you nowhere, like I said before, "Love yourself and be glad you still alive." It's best to be happy with who you are than to be mad at the next person because of who they are. You shouldn't want hate in your heart, I mean I don't and I know I'm not going to hate just because someone is doing better than me or happier than me. What imma try to do is try my best to find a way to make me happy and stay away from hating, sad, mad and bitterness as much as possible just to please God. I'm going to ask God, "Will you please bring me happiness, Lord?" You best to believe happiness is coming and it might not come when you want it but it when it does, it's going to feel so good! Don't forget to thank God when it do come…you have to give God the Glory!

5.9.14

Thinking in Prison

Today was a very blessed day for me…I ran 2 ½ miles and did 600 squats and ran some more… lol. The reason why I'm going so hard is because hard work pays off in the end. When leave prison I want to ready for the runway, my next photo shoot, acting gig, school and life all over again. For now I'm just chillin and thanking God for all He has done for me and the energy I have to workout like I do…to me it's a blessing. I know when I do get out I'm going to put my kids to work with this running ima be doing, even my lil girl. I hope they are ready because they love to work out with me, so ima get them right. I know I talk about God a lot when I write and whoever may be reading this would say, "Dang, he talk about God a lot." I do that because He has been so good to me and he brightens me up at times when I might wanna feel down and I love it! So, I have to give Him the glory as much as I can.

5.10.14

Thinking in Prison

Today is 5-10-14, a pretty, cool day for me so for…I took some pics today to send home to my kids and my mom…her B-day is coming up at the end of the month, so I sent out some love…I was seating here looking at the pics my baby momma sent me of my kids and then I put the pics beside the pics I took today and was saying dang I have some beautiful kids and they have a dad with a strong mind and good heart. I'm so glad they have a dad like me that's going to do my very best to be there in their life as much as I can. I know I'm in prison now, but I can say I have been there for them every since they came out the pussy, but when I get out we gone have so much fun. I know they are missing me like crazy that's why I had to send them a pic to let them know that daddy is OK, I will be home as soon as they open them gates for me. I love them/my kids so much and wanna show them a better life then what I had. That's my goal in life is to get this money and show them the world. I miss my oldest son, T Dog Jr., but I know God is going to keep on blessing him until we meet again and I do believe that we will see that day. I went out to reck today to get a lil workout in and me and my dawg was talking and I was telling him that if I was to ever come back to prison again imma make sure I have a chick there to really ride with me and show me mad love and he was telling me that I need a white girl. I told him that the white girls be telling me that I don't look like I talk to white girls. I told him that I have talked to 1 or 2 before and all they do is look at my pics on Facebook and say I look like I think I'm all that. They just scared to holla at me for some reason. I think they think all I wanna do is hurt their feelings, but that's not the case all I be wanting to do is see way the love at and see if we can vibe, but they don't see it like that. I have had women tell me that I look to good and they don't want me to hurt their feelings they rather an ugly dude or an alright dude hurt them not a cute or good looking dude lol that's fucking crazy! I asked my homie what do I do to make them feel me and he told me to just keep being me, but he did tell me that I have a demeaner about myself that say I have no feelings, but I told him I do have feelings, things hurt me I just know how to get over it and he tells me that I am very strong and I should get a tat that say 'untouchable' lol I'm thinking about it too. He said I just have to get somebody that understands me that's all because to me I am a very loving person, but I can see bullshit if it's there and I know how to just chill if I see bullshit. All at the same time I still show love…about prison I damn sho' aint trying to come back ever! To all the white or black women just so yall know I like all women.

5.20.14

Why I Don't Look In the Mirror That Much

My reasons for not looking in the mirror that much is, what am I looking for is the question…smh. No, I don't think I'm ugly or don't like to look at myself. It's just I am a male and I feel like if I have to keep looking in the mirror like that, I feel like I might look at myself and find a reason not to like my outside look. So, what I do is I might check myself out every no and then, but always in the mirror like a girl is not me. What I do is, I really live for God! He has me shining like a bright light. By me doing that I really feel like you don't even have to look in the mirror that much about whatever you do and everything will work out for you. Not only that I see how people look at me and that's how I'm able to tell how I look. Some call me cute, some may call me peanut head dude, but to me I'm that dude! The reason I say that is I try my best to do right; one thing I know is if you also take care of yourself as much as you can you won't really have a problem about how you look. I'm not saying to don't look at yourself, all I'm saying is a female do not want a dude that's always looking at his damn self (shhit, to me it's a sign of being gay). Some dudes love to look at themselves and will say gay shit like they would date themselves, but for me I do it for the ladies. I keep a nice cut, keep my teeth clean and stay fresh and the ladies love it. Now that I'm in prison I really don't look at myself that much because they make us shave everything off our face. So, to me I really don't feel like the real T Dog. I feel like I look like a fuckin inmate so there's no need to always be looking in the mirror like that when I know I look like a fuckin shave bird lol, on the inside I know I look like a million bucks! I like looking at women not my damn self! Being in prison how I know I'm still on point is because the officers here still lookin' at a nigga and I can tell by the look on their face that I might be something, I doubt if a nigga is ugly. Some of the women like I say will tell me, I have a very nice smile and I'm not saying they want me all I'm saying is I try to stay on point. Some of the dudes in here will look in the mirror all the time and try to pass it to me, but I tell them I don't look in the mirror, I just go… even if I did look in the mirror I look pass my outside appearance. I see the person I'm really am and that is a good dude with a heart so big. In prison niggas know you the shit jut like you know you the shit and they be hatin bad and what I can by that is some dudes that cut hair will hate so bad to where they will fuck your haircut up just so you want be on point and looking good. What I do is walk with confidence and keep a smile on my face and say fuck getting a hair cut. When I do that and don't cut my hair they be thinking they done won, but I eventually have to get a haircut and when I do you should see their fuckin faces. Niggas be having their head down looking mad, sad and all I can do is shake my fuckin head like look at these pussy niggas…it's crazy! When I get out of this place I'm still not going to look in the mirror like that, I'm going to leave that for the ladies… I'm just not on looking at myself like that, but like I say I will check to see if I have something up my nose or check how I look with what I just put on before I step out to go somewhere, but just looking at my fuckin face saying damn I'm handsome though (I'm not on that looking in the mirror type of time in prison) I leave that for the pretty boys lol. I love me some me though and the reason I say that is because I'm so real to myself… I don't try to be nobody but my fuckin self.

5.23.14

Jesus Is Real

    The reason why I can say Jesus is real is because when I look back at my life, I can see that it was already planned. After going to all the foster homes me and my brothers have been to was all God's plan with our life. Even before the foster homes, even with our mom…God took us from our mom because at the time we was with her and time was a lil hard for her, she still wanted to be young (God seen that). By putting us under someone else care would better for us, so that we can try to have a better life…Even though it was other homes we went to, it still was a lot better than living with our mom, while, she was young and using drugs and on top of that God knew her attitude and at the time it was bad… Now I can't say when me and my brothers did stay with our mom that she treated us bad or didn't feed us. I do remember one house where we stayed at, we had a lot of food in the box. At this other house it was this truck that use to, stop by and mom and dad would buy seafood, but the food was really for them. We would still snick in the box and get some…Shhhit, we was bad like that. As I look back I feel like DCF didn't take us from our mom because she was mistreating us, they took us because she wouldn't stop using drugs is what I believe because they be wanting to do random drug screens. I know my mom attitude. Shhit, she feel like she is doing everything that they want her to do and they still want to run her life…As she would feel like. What she did was told our dad that she is giving him all the rights to us and she did! Our dad tried to get us and of course, they made him do a lot to get us, but only in the end to tell him he can't get us. He was only able to get our brother being that after taking a blood test our one brother was the only one that went back to him. He was the only one that went with our dad; the rest of us went to foster care. Like I said, I'm very thankful and grateful too! God saved us and even though we were taken and went to homes where we learned things in life that could help us, if we were to use them. For me, one of the homes I was to we worked in the fields all the time. After I left there we went to a home that was more laid back, but all at the same time we had things around the house that we had to do. Like, taking out the trash, keeping the yard clean and going to church, all of these things were cool because even though we chose to do other things like the street shit, we still had learned these good qualities in life. They're going to be with us for the rest of our life. The good part about it we can teach our kids these same good qualities, the reason I say I'm grateful is because I'm still alive after all I feel like I have been through. My kids are alive and healthy, my mom is still alive, and I'm good and healthy. We still have hope to do better in life and I'm so grateful for it all. I have never been shot, I seen all my kids be born, all my brothers are still alive, and no one close to me has died yet. This is my first and last time to prison; I have a good heart and won't let anything get in my way from receiving my Blessings from God. I'm smart; a lot of people love me, but I do know a lot of them hate me. I'm just grateful for my lil life and I'm just glad I know God and have Him in my life also. Without Him ain't no telling where I would be. He is the one that have me so strong and strong-minded and all that I have been through I'm just grateful to still be alive. He keeps me in a good mood no matter where I'm at. He is real and I know because he saved me and he will do the same for you. Now, there is a few things I can talk about that do bother me if I get to thinking to long…All the real I have done, all the being nice and being there for my mom (like for her Birthday) or letting my kids be apart of her and her boyfriend life. Now that I'm in prison she is not really there for me or any of her own kids (4 boys). I mean, she love my kids because I brought them around a lot so she could know some of her grandkids as much as she can. All at the same time at least she can get her life together so she can help be there for there dad. Like send me some money or try to come see me or something! Don't let me just sit and prison and do the time by myself…She have sent me a Birthday card and she do speak when my baby momma write me and tell me, but still as a child the kid be wanting more. The reason why I might be feeling this way is because I'm locked up and may be in my feelings a lil or maybe not. Shhit, if you are a parent and your kids are still alive believe you me they still need you in ways you would never think of. My goals are: to stop getting in trouble, stay out of jail and prison and be there for my kids as much as I can. If I have to stop doing this or that and one of my kids need me I'm going to try my hardest to be right there with them to make them feel loved. I know right now I might be in prison, but all at the same time I do have a plan to do better with my life. For myself and my kids so I can teach them the things they need to know and tell them that daddy has been places they don't want to go. I'm going to let them know that being bad is not good. It will get you no where but a bad spot in your life...I can say the time I have been around them I have put them up on a lot and we have had a lot of fun times. (I have been there for them). As they get older I'm going to let them know where I have been and what I been through, so they will understand daddy and let them know not to be like me but better than me and to stay in school because they don't want to be lost in this world with no dreams. It's best to stay on track now and they want have to worry about the bullshit.

5.28.14

Prison Time

I hit my cousin up the other day...Not knowing if he was going to pick up the phone, but he did. I had someone to call him and let him know that I was in prison. As soon as the person called my cousin for me and let him know I was in prison, shhit in like three days my cousin had me a letter in the mail. The first letter was him just reaching out to me, to see if I was getting his mail and I was. If felt so good to hear from him and not only that what I did was when I wrote him back, I asked him for something, not just to see what he'll say but to see if he would really be there for me. I remember when my cousin was living here in Florida and we would chill or if we would talk over the phone, he would tell me about this person or one of his long time friends he let me meet (after being in prison). My cousin use to work to a prison till he got in a fight with one of the dudes he was working with, but I say that to say this now that I'm in prison and he now know that I'm here I wanted to see if he don't mind being there for me. My reason I really want him here for me is because I know he is a real nigga. Even though he never been to prison, but when I was young, he would tell me how cool he would be to the inmates when he did work to the prison. I needed him to be there for me because my flaw ass baby momma done stopped writing me because she said she didn't like my last letter. I wrote her, but she has not wrote in three months so now that I'm in touch with my cousin I really don't care to hear from her like that. I asked her to send me pics or just to keep in touch and this bitch want to act like my letter was so fuckin bad or disrespectful. All I told her in the letter is if she don't bring the kids to see me, I'm going to feel like I don't have kids. Now she not knowing what I'm going through with first baby momma because I didn't tell her and the reason, I didn't tell her is because I felt like she would want to try some bullshit too, just like she is now. So I keep it to myself, but what gets me is 2nd baby momma was writing me when I first got to prison feeling sad and shit, letting the kids write me telling me how the kids miss me and how my three year old is being bad in school because he misses his daddy. I'm only an hour away from my baby momma and it's not that hard to get here so what I do is send her a visitation form and she sent it back. So now she can come see me, so after she tell me about my son being bad in school, I tell her to bring him to see me then. I know I can get in his ear and talk to him and he will listen to me and not only that all he wants to do is see his daddy to make sure I'm okay, and then he'll be okay! But noooooo she never gets the kids up here to see me so that's when I wrote the letter to her saying dang if you don't bring the kids to see me, it's going to feel like I have no kids. I know this bitch hate on me and want me to feel down about something, but I'm too strong for that. If she don't want to bring the kids to see me and its cool, I'll just wait till I get out to see them. What I did was took some pictures and sent them one and my momma one and after that I haven't heard anything from no one. After I read her letter again about my son being bad in school, I seen that she told me that she was going to put the boys in T-ball and he can take his anger out on that lol, so now that I'm thinking I should have told her yea that would be a very good idea and left it like that. I hit her up one time after that and asked her to put some money on my books and she did, but like I say these bitches think they are making me hurt, but there not. I just feel sorry for my kids because when I get my money back right and move on don't say I didn't try and you can go get them a new daddy, if you feel that's best for them. I'm going to put some money in the bank for my kids, so they'll know I cared and moved on with my life. I know it's my fault that I'm here, but baby momma tells me she want to be friends so I tell her okay. That's not what I wanted, but if she wants that then I have to give it to her and that's what I did. I'm thinking she going to bring the kids lol shhit not!! But the thing is I'm not hurting at all I just feel sorry that my kids might have to wait for me to get out to see them. What I do is pray for them and ask God to please keep them safe, happy and to keep me in their heart. If I do talk to my baby momma again, I'm not going to say anything about my kids I'm going to just stay to myself. Don't get me wrong I still got love for the bitch because I done been with this hoe for 8 years and have these 3 kids from this hoe, but it's like I love my kids but I really don't want nothing to do with them, because of their mom and how she been trying to keep them away mentally. All these or some of these bitches do is care about themselves and want a nigga to be up their azz, but bitch you got me fucked up. I love you but I'm not dumb for ya azz. I can move on just like she can and not only that I know that I'm the best at everything that I do. The ladies love me, I'm a real nigga and I do real nigga shit. So once I find me that right bad, crazy, bad bitch, and she loyal, I'll be good. What she better hope is she get a nigga better than me and that's going to be hard. That's why I want my cousin to be here for me so I want have to ask her for shit and I'm moving on her azz. The thing about it all I forgive the bitch because in real life I'm not hurting real talk. One thing I know about bitches that wants to be nasty is they want you to need them, but I'm going to play it cool for now til I get back hot then I'm going to turn up on her azz and really act like I don't care… (about shit!). I won't ask to see my kids ever, I ain't going to ask her for shit when I get out because if you're not here now I'm not going to need you when I do get out. This bitch think I ain't gone power back up like I'm dead or something, but bitch you got me fucked up. I'll never give up on my life so whoever hoping I stay down and not come back up, ya'll in trouble like a motherfucker. I asked my cousin for some books and some money and he told me that he gone handle all that and I asked him to hook me up with a female around his way baby and if he do hook me up with a pretty nice chic it's going to be really on. Ain't no telling how things are going to work out with me and the female, all I know is I'm trying to treat her like somebody also I'm letting her know that I have goals and I hope that she does too. If not, I'll try to help her in ways if I can, but I also learn that you have to be carful how you help people that come in your life and the reason I say that is because that's how I feel like I messed up with my 2nd baby momma. She would tell me about her life and how her mom treated her and how they didn't get alone and how her dad really wasn't there for her like he was there for her brother and sister. It was like she was an outcast of the family and by her telling me these things I started to feel sorry for the girl. My heart went out to her, so now I see why she didn't want to go back home to her mom, but what I use do was tell her to at least call her mom. So, her mom would know where she was, but she never cared to do that, but she did. Like I say we would go and get her clothes then back to my place. I say that to say you have to watch because by me showing her this love and feeling sorry for her made me not like her mom or dad. In my head I felt like why would you treat your child like this and she is your first lil girl…crazy! So, after I meet her mom for some reason her mom didn't like me and it feel like she didn't because her daughter found someone that could love her the right way. I was there for her I just wanted to be her friend also, not rushing things as far as a relationship. At the time I had another female that was in love with me, not only that I was in the streets living my life. I somehow still had a heart when it came down to hurting people, so once I seen or knew her mom didn't care for me like that, I didn't care for her like that either. After the accident with our son and my son had to go live with her I was very mad because I knew that her mom didn't like me. It was going to be hard to see my son more than one time a week because she told DCF that she didn't want me to her house and things like that (that fucked me up with seeing my son to her house). The only way I was able to see him was at the Center for an hour and every time my son would come, we would play, but when it was time to leave he didn't understand why he couldn't go with me. He would take it out on me, I felt so bad for us in these times in our life. Me and my son was so close and when he had to stay with her mom by me knowing a lil bit about her mom and how she did my baby momma, I was very upset that he had to stay with her till I got done with a case plan. My baby momma could go over there and visit him but, I know with my baby momma mom not liking me and then not liking her own daughter like that, I knew she wasn't going to really be feeling my son like that because he look just like me. So, what if he's her grandson, this lady was mad at the world and all she really had was her kids. Her man left her and that's her kids dad that she was with, so being that all she had was her kids and for me to come in and take one of her girls out her house she wasn't with that shit! What she did was made it hard for me because what she was doing is turning my son against me and whatever way she could and in a way she did it. One day we had to go to court and I was mad I couldn't get my son back and I had an attitude out this world and after we left out the courtroom, I cussed her out so bad till today I want to tell her sorry for how I acted that day in the courtroom, because it was bad! I was calling her all kinds of names as I was leaving the courthouse and the thing was, I was doing it for me and my baby mom for how she didn't like me for no reason and for mistreating her daughter. I say that was the wrong way to go about things, but I was still young at the time and my attitude was still bad. That's why I have to watch how I want to help people because in the end it might bite you in the ass. I was trying to give her love that I knew she was missing, but all at the same time I couldn't do that. As time went on, I saw that she still wanted love from her mom and dad. While I was out there her and her mom still didn't get alone, and her mom was so mean to her till our son don't even want or like to go back over there. As a matter of fact our son use to see how mean his grandma was to his mom, so now I'm in prison I feel like my baby momma done seen her mom be so mean and want more in life till I feel like my baby momma getting her mom ways. What I mean is picking up her mom ways wanting more out of life now that I'm down bad as far as money. Now she wants to find every reason to not want to be with T Dog lol. She (baby momma) say that I put my hands on her, but when I had money, she would put her hands on me and now she sees I hit back. Now it's me put my hands on her, now that I'm broke… bitch I'm not crazy, I don't just go around putting my hands on bitches, ya'll want to play games and don't want a nigga to do shit about it and when a nigga do oh he put his hands on me lol (why?) My reason is that she knows I love my kids and she want to play them pussy ass games and act like she wants to have or let my kids stay in my life. Then she wants to act like she wants to take them away, bitch you are doing to fuckin much playing with me and my kid's feelings (you got me fucked up). I'm not the one to be played with, so I guess we might need to move on because I do want me a real woman that's going to love me and love that I love my kids and not going to play with me or my kids feelings. Some nasty people like to find out strong people weaknesses and wait for the right time to want to try them. You would think she would be happy that I want to be there for my kids, but shhit these bitches don't care. You know why she don't care is because she wants all the love for herself because she might feel like she is missing love from all the right people in her life. So now that she was blessed to have kid's she want to try to make them feel like she is the best, but my kids know their dad and they know their mom. All at the same time they love us both. I just don't kiss ass to make them love daddy, I teach them the right way of life and they love and respect me for it. When they do see me, I know they are going to be so happy and I'm going to be happy to see them too. When they are away from their mom, they act so much different, but when we all together they really don't care to see us vibe. My lil girl damn sho' play a big part of us not vibin, only on my baby momma side tho. Not from me because I knew what they was trying to do. For me it was not working, I would make their ass go watch TV or play with them, get them ready for bed and vibe with baby momma. I'm telling you kids are something, they would try to out smart you, but not me. I would get their ass right and let them know me and your momma love each other and that's what it's going to be. So ya'll asses might as well be happy and smile big. It talks about these types of things in the Bible as well, how kids will be with their parents and it's crazy!

I'm not letting them stop my happiness and when they get older I won't stop theirs. I will help them as much as I can and if they love that person to try and work it out. I know as they get older they'll understand more about life, they just kids now. I'm the one don't mind getting their mind on the right track before hand. Shit crazy with me and the kids I done had, like I say I use to want a lot of kids. Now I'm like "fuck that" these bitches play too many games and they wonder why they asses be laid up dead somewhere in the fuckin woods. I'm just not the one that's going to kill their ass. I'm going to kill them like this, I'll act like I don't give a damn and then pray for them and ask God to love my kids for me because I have to go live my life.

Real Life

Now what made me want to do the modeling and acting is my big cousin. He will tell about all the money people made doing this, I'm thinking to myself like, "Damn, they making that much money" and cuz was like, "Yeah." He went on naming all of the actors like Denzel Washington, Jamie Foxx, Will Smith, Ice Cube and many more…I started to think like, "Damn, I want to make money like that, not only that I want to be a star." Shhit, I want to be somebody and I want to see the world, the only way I will do that is trying something new (acting/modeling). What I did was started to work out hard so my body will be on point, then I did my first photo shoot and it turned out good and when everybody seen the pictures a lot of people liked them. From then I just kept doing photo shoots and every time I got better with each shoot… Its fun, it's different and I meet a lot of important people, ithere are a lot of pretty women and a lot of people look at you different when you tell them what you do for a living. It makes me feel real good to tell somebody that I model and act then to be telling them I'm still a street nigga… The things I want in life I can't get by being a street nigga so I had to change the game up and look for another way out the hood. My most important thing is I will love to do is be in my kids life as much as possible. I want to start while they are young so I can teach them as much as I can about life and keep them in church as much as

I can so they will know God as much as I do. I know it will help them in life to know God then being in the streets or just being around their Mom all the time because to me a mom can only be a mom, not their Dad! The mom can never take a dad place or her new boyfriend. She needs to let the real dad be apart of their kids life (if the dad wants to be there). That's what I been going thru my whole time I been having kids. The baby mommas want to either be hateful or keep me away or they want to play mom and the dad to the kids. Like I say, "A mom can't be their dad," I mean she can be there for her child as much as she can, but that child is still missing someone and that's their dad. I give it to the women that is there for the kids that have to play both parents because their dad don't want to step up to the plate. I respect that, but for the women to plain out take kids out their fathers' life that is very selfish and mean. Now this kid has to feel all kinds of ways because the mom done filled the kids head up with all kinds of lies about their dad. Knowing that the kid dad love his child and want to be there, but the mom want let him...now don't get me wrong there are some dads out there that don't give a fuck about kids or there own kids, but there are still some good dads out there (I'm one of them). What I have been seeing is these women having babies from their baby daddies and instead of staying together they break up, get another man and then his dumb ass wants to play daddy to the woman kids. Which is another man kids and the mother of the child don't even know how bad their child is hurting because they can't be around their real dad. What the kids have to do is start to like the new boyfriend (the mom have) and if they stay together over two years or so then the kids starts calling the new boyfriend daddy because his real daddy is nowhere to be found. Not only that the new dude/boyfriend already have kids of his own that his azz can't even see his damn self, but now he want to play daddy to another man kids like he is a good dude or something. Fuck nigga you are a sucker if you ask me! If a woman have kids and they never go with their dad, to me it's something wrong with that picture so me I'll look into why their kids don't go with their dad. Once I find out then that's when I know if I want to keep talking to her or not (Real Shit! T Dog).

6.7.14

Thinking in Prison

Sitting here thinking about when I stayed with my Grandma and when I started to sing in the choir at church…the songs were nice and some of them was pretty cool. Now that I'm older and I'm singing them I understand them a whole lot better. Now when I sing some of the songs something come over me as I'm singing them and it's so beautiful! Today I was singing, "Hold on a Change Is Coming." Now I really understand that song. Like back in the days when I song that song it was just a song that was picked for us to sing. Someone in the choir asked the kids to lead the song and that kid was me and one of my foster cousins. I can say the older people that were there really enjoyed us singing that song. I don't know if it was because we were young and singing or they knew what all the songs meant, it could have been both. All I know is when we would sing it the church would get a lil up beat with that song. Now that I'm here in prison on Sundays I don't do the things I love to do like workout, I just chill out and give God most of my time and give Him thanks. I try my best to give God Sunday for His day so today I was singing some church songs and it just came over me on how I really understand a lot of the words more. The songs "Thank you, Lord," and "People get ready cause the train is coming." These are some of the songs that came to me while I was having a lil church to myself at work. I could feel the presence of the Lord all over me till I started to tear up. After I got off from work I went to the Rec Yard I ran into one of my homies and he had an mp3 player, while I was talking to him he was listening to it. He took it out of his ear and told me to listen but before he could place it in my hand I told him, "I don't want to no slow music." When I started to listen, it was church music he was listening to and it ended up being a song I already knew. After the song I was going to give it back but he was like, "Listen to this one," and as I started to listen I told him, "Church songs makes me cry" and he was like, "Yea because we are living everything they are saying." When the song started and as I listened it was that song, "Break Every Chain." He tells me, "He was about to hit the chow line." I was going to go with him till the song really started and then I told him, "I wanted to take a walk by myself for a minute." That song hit me so hard till I started crying and thinking about my life and kids. I need to live how God wants me to live so I can be here for my kids, not in and out of jail and prison and just trust in Him (God) that He will make a way for me, so I can make a way for my kids. That's who I'm living for right now is my kids. I know they need me more than anyone and I want to be here for them, so they can have a better life than I did. I must say that I got off a bad start but I'm going to make up for everything I missed while being in prison. Nobody said it will be easy but I don't believe He brought me this far to leave me…I can't say that it won't be hard, but ima do my very best, my very best is a whole lot because I go hard. The thing about me is I want my kids to have more than I had and to me I had a lot. When I went to the streets I brought any and everything I wanted, even things for them. This time I want to get these things the right way, that way I can get things for them and not worry about the cops or goin back to jail or prison. I can stay in their life and watch my kids enjoy every bit of life, that's my goal is to make their life a whole lot easier than mine. I can do all things with God in my life and doing the right things.

6.11.14

Thinking in Prison

Thinking to myself about life…my life: I can't say it is or was that bad but, at the same time it's a lot of stress behind it all…I was thinking, I have four brothers none of them really had or have anything to offer the next brother. My mom is 55 and she still use drugs and not only that she don't have nothing to offer non of her kids (boys) and that's me and my brothers. We been asking and waiting our Mom to stop using drugs since we was kids and she have not given us that yet…Do we want her stop using drugs? Well, I can only speak for myself right now. I did and still do because I care for her health and being that I have brought my kids in her life, I want her to try and live a log time if it's God's will…I can't say how all my brothers feel about our mom, all I can say is our older brother and our Mom didn't get alone to well because they both have bad attitudes, so my older brother stayed away a lot. My brother that's two years younger than me just got out of prison, but I can't really say how he feels about our Mom. All I know is he got out of prison he stopped by our Moms house looking for me and my baby mom. Momma told him that now I'm in prison…Our younger brother just had got out of prison for doing like 2 years, maybe stayed out for a year or so and not to long went back for 15 years. When he first went to prison I wasn't in prison yet, he wrote our Mom a letter but, when I got over to her house she gave it to me to read. I waited til I got to my crib to read it; the letter was saying he wanted her in his life and how he wish she was there for him when he was younger. I mean it was a lot of lil things that my younger brother wished he had dealing with our Mom. As I'm reading the letter I'm shaking my head like shhit brah I feel ya but, what you want is the same thing we all been waiting ever since we been growing up. Now that you are in prison what you are asking for it's going to be far too hard to get because this lady is already a trip…she might love us all but, if you are not around doing good things in her life and making her smile shhit, Momma gonna put ya azz on the back rack…Now two of my brothers like the oldest and the youngest have lived with our Mom while they have been older and they have done some fucked up shit, like steal or take her boyfriend things (clothes), lil things they would lie about doing it is what mad Momma mad at them so much: versus me that have lived there and was able to help out and always had my own besides a place to stay. I had to stay with them for some time, so what would happen with me while staying there is our Mom would end up taking from me or stealing from me, then blame it on my brother or her boyfriend and lie to my face and tell me she didn't do it. Knowing damn well she did…That's the reason why she really don't have to much or nothing at all bad to say about me because I stayed out her way. I never gave her any trouble like my two brothers; she always took from me because I always had. My brothers feel like Momma like me more but, it's not like that; I don't do the shit

I do to her, when me and momma do get mad at each other I don't just leave I stay there, versus my older would leave and stay away and be just as mad has she was…I'm staying because I feel like, "Why leave when this is our only real mom?" We gone fuss and fight sometimes but I'm not going to leave and stay away like I don't care. This is our only real mom we have and I want to know her, know her ways, how she thinks and know her heart, so that's why I stay. I believe that's why we get alone so well because I won't get so mad and stay away. One time I did and put her on punishment and stayed away for a year just to show her I can stay away and will if I want. That's not what ima do, ima just give you a lil time to think about what you did to your son then I'll come back and I do…not saying my other brothers don't know her, maybe they just don't feel like dealing with the BS when it comes down to fussing a lil bit with her. As for my mom sisters and brothers they all are dying at a young age. I be telling or asking my mom to slow down with the drugs and drinking so she can at least live to get older. She have been using for some time now, ever since we was young boys…yes she is grown but, all at the same time we would like to see our Mom live a lot longer than she thinks. I would hate for my kids to see their Grandma die young and she is the only Grandma they have been around that love them so much. The way I see it is I'm trying to save all of us from a sad day…I mean while I been in prison and two of my Aunts have passed, its' sad to hear about that happening. I also know they lived a hard life but, I think they would say they went out with a bang because I know my two aunts knew they were sick. They were so gone on drugs and life, I really don't think they even cared even more so they lived on the edge…as far as all of their kids they left behind I can't really say how they all are doing, all I can say is I hope they are trying their best to do better than their mom. As for me I'm trying to do better than my whole family, not to be better than anyone but, to do better so I can rep for our family. We all can rep for each other but, being that we all never grew up around each other a lot of them hate on the next, when we all need to come together. The only time is when someone in the family has died and when we do that we still don't really talk. I've heard my cousin tell me that the reason why some of my cousins are mad at me is because I said I'm not keen to them…I'm like way the hell this come from but, she wasn't able to tell me. What I think is that's there excuse for being mad that we didn't grow up around them and they are so mad about that. They are so mad that even though I am keen to them, I don't act like them at all. What I mean about that is some of them have some very nasty ways about themselves…and they get a lot of their ways growing up around their mom or dad or just their mom, so what they did was followed the leader but, as far as me and my brothers we was blessed enough to not to be around that. That's why I say, "I won't complain." The foster homes that I've been to was not like my biological family and that's a good thing…Grandma always stayed clean, always had a nice car, taught us to always do right. As I got older those things stayed with me and as far as my real family, people from town talked bad about them saying to me, "Baby, you look like your family." I would smile every time someone would know that I'm a related to my biological family. They also would say, "I hope you are nothing like them" and I would tell them, "I'm not, I'm different, I'm not nasty, I'm a good kid trying to make a way for myself." My family have had it so hard I feel like I have to come up and rep as hard as I can for all my family. That's what I'm going to do. I feel like God created us for a reason. In my head he wanted us to dream big, be better, and love one another no matter what. I'm going to try my best to do that. As far as my brothers, I love them. It's been so long since all of us been around each other and not only that we all been locked up. When one is getting out another one is going in, so all I can say is, "I'm going to try and keep in contact with them." I still be thinking to myself about how my brothers are as a person and what I mean about that is I be feeling they be waiting on me to get sack, so they can come up off me. All at the same time shhit I be needing help my damn self but, I can say we all have helped each other out the best way we could so, I'm thankful. My oldest brother, I really can't say about dude and the reason why I say that is because since dude has got his lil girlfriend he feels like he have the world and don't need nobody else in life. I don't like that about him…to me that's some fuck shit, only fuck niggas will act and do fuck shit like he do. After all we have been through he want to act like he don't have to talk to his family cause he got his lil woman, bitch shit if you ask me.

6.14.14

Drugs I Use to Sell

Me selling drugs is something I jumped into because I was around it and not only that it was fast money. Not really thinking clear but, now that I'm older I think back to all the drugs I use to sell like, crack cocaine, x-pills and coke. One of the main drugs that stand out to me is crack. The reason why it stands out is because that's the drug my mom use, that's the drug so bad in ways a lot of people can't get off of…that's the same drug that most of all my moms sisters is on and that's the drug I use to sell…I'm I wrong for doing it? Not at the time because all I seen was the money, crack would make anybody do anything back when I was selling it. When I did end up getting around my mom, she would want me to sell it to her and it's not that I really wanted to but, what she would do is tell me if I don't sell it her she's going to go and get it from the next dope boy so I might as well get the money, so sometimes I would and sometimes I would just give it to her because I didn't want her to ask no body else for no dope. The way my mom would tell me is how she would see things it was cool how she would lay it down to me. Telling me that crack don't kill nobody, but what she was doing was keeping me off her back about it and all at the same time I never seen it kill nobody myself. I just know the people that use it would do anything for it or to have it. I never seen no one die from it, so one time I was in our county jail and was talking to this dude and he was telling me that crack do kill you and I'm like for real and he was like yeah, it fuck with your heart and at the same time he was in jail with me telling me all the pills he had to take. Some of the reasons was for crack, so in my head I'm thinking like my mom is a fuckin trip! She be telling me all this just so she won't have to stop smoking that shit. All I can say is, "She grown." Like, she always told me, "When God get her to stop she will." Now that I'm older and aware of the drugs, that's one drug I care less to sell. I don't care to sell no drugs but crack is one I don't want to sell and I'm not going to sell. It's a lot of things I never really paid too much attention to when I was in the streets because at the time my life was going so fast. I didn't really see a lot or noticed everything I needed too really pay attention to. I was just livin'…life was okay but now it's time for a better life without the selling of the drugs.

6.14.14

Thinking in Prison --- Livin' 4 My Kids

In my heart my kids are my everything! That's including God also, but not only my kids is all I love; I love all kids…my reason for feeling this way is because I remember being a lil kid and I wanted a lot of love myself and I did get it. The only thing about that is it wasn't from the people I felt like was suppose to be loving me (like my mom or my dad). It still was cool because the love I did end up getting was good still. I was cool with it and it kept my mind off of other things, like who I wanted to be there loving on me. I use to want a lot of kids until I made one and my baby momma started to play with my son being in my life. After that I still had more, but I asked the second baby momma will she play with me with my kids if I had any from her and she told me, "No, she wouldn't." lol ☺ shhit…After my first son with her came the bullshit and I still gave her two more kids after our first son…It's crazy! My first baby momma already had a son when I got with her and one day I ended up going to her church with a woman that lived in the hood where I was living with my homeboy, sister and mom. She asked me will I go to church with her and I said yea…so when I get to the church I didn't now who church it was besides the lady who asked me to come, but when I get there I see all these females and I'm like damn! It's a lot of girls to this church, so I have a seat and I noticed my first baby momma went to this church also. Now, she wasn't my baby momma at this point, but I did have her number by this time so I'm saying to myself like damn, this girl go to this church; so I noticed her but I also see all these other girls. All I wanted was lil red and that's my baby momma #1. After church the lady asked me did I want to go out to eat with her, I told her yes we can do that. Everybody at the church ended up going out to eat, so now I'm seating at the table with the church all these females, the lady that I rode with and the lil red I was liking (#1 baby momma). So as I'm seating to the table me and baby momma keep catching eye contact because we already had done meet, but nobody know this but me and her. So we eat and after we was done I paid for the meal like a gentlemen and as we were walking out of the place I notice my baby momma lil boy and some how me and him just bonded for some reason. He ended up coming to me and I picked him up; and why did I do that ☺. Lil man did not want me to put him down and didn't want to go back to his mom, granddad or grandma. He was stuck to me and I don't know why…as I'm holding lil man he was just chillin, but if somebody tried to grab him he would pull back like he didn't know them and I'm just laughing like damn kid you can't go with me. At the same time I was still young myself with no kids but this kid didn't want to leave my arms. Now all the lil ladies is noticing this and they are so surprised about it, but also looking at baby momma like girl what you gone do because your son is crazy about this dude, so I gave lil man to his mom and I have a lil talk with her all at the same time, but still nobody know that I know her, so I think I told her I'll hit her up later. Now I'm back in the car with the lady and we are headed back to the hood, with me not knowing this lady is feeling me too! We get to her crib and I start fucking her too, now I'm fucking her all the time. I started to fuck my baby momma too, but one time I didn't have no place to sex my baby momma so I take her to the lady apartment to sex her and this day after fucking her for some time I wanted my own child. Before I put my dick in her I asked her, "Will she have my kid?" and she told me, "yes." I fucked her real good in the lady house on the floor, now this lady wasn't my lady or girlfriend she was just a woman that was feeling me and didn't mind giving me the pussy and I didn't mind getting it! She knew me and my baby momma had a thing for each other from the day we went out to eat, but she didn't care. She don't know I sexed my baby momma at her crib and still don't know. I put a baby in baby momma that day and she pushed out a lil boy at 2lbs 8oz after that baby boy shit started getting crazy with me and her. We was cool for a lil while, then when I moved out shit got crazier and crazier with our son. I asked her to have my baby because before we had my son I was there with her son and the lil man liked me like crazy. Being that she seen that her son was crazy about me I thought it would be nice to have a son of my own, after my first son was in and out of my life I was sad, mad and feeling some type of way. After time went on I meet baby momma #2, now before baby momma #2 I had two other females I was messing with that wanted a baby from me, but the whole time I'm fuckin them no baby…now it wasn't that I was trying to make a baby with these females at the time it was I was fuckin with them for some time and I didn't mind if they popped up with a baby, but they didn't! Nan one of them…I mean one did popped up with a baby, but the baby died. Then the other one had a baby, but it wasn't mine. I was crying when I found out that the baby wasn't mine not just because of the baby, but because I liked her and she liked me too. I had so much going on with females to where me and her split up for some time and when I hit her back up she had a baby on the way. Some type of way I was thinking it might have been mine and she let me think that it was mine for a lil bit till she got mad at me one day and told me it wasn't lol. I was mad too; we stopped talking after that. The other female that had my baby and the baby dies at five months, I cried about the baby dying, but it's all good. Still in my heart I wanted more kids and that's when I meet my second my baby momma and still have had a rough time bonding with the kids. I love them in my heart so, so much and I love kids that I come in contact with that are not even mine. I mean me and the kids that I don't know love me so much and my own kids is the ones I be having the problems with, I don't know why they want to take me through the bullshit but they do. God bless them all, all my baby mommas I wish yall the best, but just so yall know I'm the best father for all my kids. To all the kids out there that their dad is not around I just want to say be strong, live life the best way you know, keep God in your life no matter what and He'll make a way for you. As for my kids daddy gone be here for you as much as I can and if I'm not there just know that I'm praying for yall every night, every minute and I know God will bless ya'll.

6.17.14

Livin 4 My Kids Continued

Today I was feeling kind of down…thinking about my kids, but really my oldest son is what really was on my mind. It's like I can be hard a lot of times but deep down in my heart I'm really, really hurting in my heart about me not being able to vibe with my son like I always wanted too. I been hard for a long time, but all I can think about is how I miss my son and when I have been around him the things we have talked about just be coming up in my head and don't nobody know what me and him have talked about but, me and him. He was telling me a lot about ho he felt about his brother, mother and her new husband and he would tell me that his brother would be mean to him, how his mom want let him come around me or how his mom husband get up on him asking him do he want to fight and shit. These are the things my son have told me about them and I only see him or have seen him like every once in awhile that's when he would call me out the blue and ask me to come to a football game or to see him light fireworks and I would come! After that I won't see him for a long time, I don't understand why but now my biggest heart break is my son calling another dude daddy when my son already has a dad and that's me! After we did the court thing and his name has been changed and my son is calling dude dad some type of way I feel like my son is dead. It's like he's been taking away from me but still alive and it really hurt for someone you love to be somewhere he don't want to be, but forced to be there, has to call someone else daddy and this nigga have his own kids to take care of. This bitch baby momma of mine had this nigga play daddy to all her kids when all her kids already have their own dad…that shit is crazy to me, but the stress it brings to me is so fucked up and have me so fucked up to where I rather be dead….it's like a pain that I can't get rid of and I don't think I ever will because I feel like as of now I know this bitch made baby momma of mine is in my son head making him feel some type of way with the help of her other son and that bitch nigga that's there…making my lil man feel left out when he is the best one over there. In my heart I rather me and him die together than for us to be apart like we are. I know people might say, "Well, T Dog Jr. when he get older he will find you and yall will be tight all over again." That's not how I see it, I want to be there now and forever fuck that older shitt! Fuck!!!! My heart is really fucking hurting and I still have three more kids to live for and I'm trying my hardest to stay strong for them, but something in me want to give up so bad and just leave. I know they love and need me to be there for them so I can't give up, but I still rather be dead because then these bitches can't hurt me then. I feel like they only do it because they know I have been there for my kids the best way ever and a lot of times people don't like the good guys they always like the bad guys. It's like I always see and read it in the books when the ladies say they like the bad guys with the pretty face, nice body, but when they get them they fuck em', have a baby from them and then want another bad guy or switch to the fuckin lame ass niggas that's going to do whatever they want…bad guys ain't having that shit. To me bad guys are the real nigga the ones that will let yo azz know that bitch I'm not a fuckin push over so don't fuckin try me! The bad guy is the one that will fuck yo friend and lie about it to yo face and tell you, "Sorry people are saying things like that baby, but it's not me." The good guys is the one that get fucked over when it comes down to the real shit when they want to be there for the git and the mom won't let them…you know why? They really want to be able to say what a nigga aint doing but they can't because the nigga so real and deep down in their heart they want the real nigga back. They already know it won't work so they rather be mean to him because they mad because he done moved on with his life to show you that it ain't no pressure. You took that from me but God will bless me with more right in front of your face. After God do that the bitch want to do more to make a nigga mad like change the kid name…all I can say is, "I put it in Gods hand." God bless!

6.19.14

Being in prison a lot of times you have a lot of mixed feelings…I do! Sometimes I'll wake up on the right side of the bed and be feeling so, so blessed. Then it be times were I'll wake up on the wrong side and be feeling stress not because I'm in here, but because my mind be playing tricks on me. I be thinking all kinds of ways, about life, my kids, my baby mommas and sometimes I be wanting to ask God, "Why do I have to go through the bullshit!" I don't, I just pay and ask God to take the evil out of my mind or I'll just go to sleep so I can stop thinking. In here all you really can do is think about all your life, your whole life at that! Sometimes it get stressful, but I thank God for putting me here (prison). It really is helping me get my mind right, it's helping me to think a whole lot better. My only thing is I don't know what's going to happen when I walk out them gates to back to my town. All I know is I have some plans that I pray that's going to work for me. Life is hard, but all at the same time you can make it a whole lot harder for yourself if you don't watch what you are doing in the streets or wherever you might be. If you don't have that role model or Jesus in your corner to save you things can go really wrong. The good thing about Jesus is He is always there for you no matter what. All you have to do is call on Him. I was feeling some type of way today about my life and my son no longer being in my life, it made me feel like I wanted to die or be dead because of the pain I had in my heart about him not being here in my life. It's my first son my Jr. and this cold hearted bitch don't want me to be apart of his life. I don't understand, when she knew I wanted to be there, but all at the same time I had to let go. So I can still live my life and that's what I did. I gave up my rights so we both can live…I already knew if I didn't do it the things that this girl would take me and my son through is not worth me fighting for my son. Then he would have to go back to her and me not knowing how she/they would treat him, people be thinking them women be so good of parents, but these bitches can be real evil! Shhit, she already one time tried to give our son to me and told me she washed her hands with him because Lil T Dog be lying, but that's not the case. Bitch you be lying on him, that boy is telling the truth about how you be treatin him, all I can say is when he get older it will all come out. When she tried to give my son to me at the time I told her no, he can stay with the both of us because he needs us both…she got my son head fucked up! It's sad to me to really know what these lil kids go through when they have these nasty ass moms…Sometimes the moms kill the child, shhit sometime the kids be wanting to kill their own parents or when they get older they (kids) act out because of what they have been through. This shit is real out here; I just pray and ask God to keep lil man safe and happy in his heart. There's one thing that I'm hoping and that's when my son do get older I hope he come back to me and when he do…Like I said before he only have one dad and that's me, so he better not bring his ass around me talking about a fuckin' step dad because I'm not hearing that shit at all. I don't give a damn how long this nigga was in your life or if your momma is still with him I don't want to hear that shit at all…I'm your fuckin dad and that's it. I can see if I never wanted to be in your life then that's different, but I was there till your fuck ass mom wanted to trip and make things hard for me…

6.21.14

Thinking in Prison

The things I brought when I was making fast money…I stayed fresh! Lots of shoes and clothes, but a lot of the things I brought like my jewelry is gone. When times got hard I pawned it, but the one thing I pawned that I went back to get dude didn't want to give it back. That was my big gold chain 325 grams is what is weighed. When I went back to get it dude told me that he sold it, but one thing I did know is he sold it before the time he was suppose to sell it. Me not really thinking clear I didn't call the police up to the pawn shop to do the police report…I almost cried in the pawn shop because I didn't know what to do, when he told me that he sold my chain. What he did was fast talk me and told me that he can get me a chain just like it by summer time. I already knew he couldn't do that because my chain was a big ass chain. It would be hard to find one like it, but he hit me with people come in here all the time and pawn chains like this. I told him "no" they don't. He told me to come back by the summer and he will have me one, so I waited until the summer and went back to his shop and guess what he brings from the back...My chain! How I knew it was mine is because it had a bend in it and I told him that this is my chain man, this is the same chain and I told him that this is my chain man. This is the same chain, but he is talking about no it's not (I knew my chain). That day I got a no trespassing at that pawn shop; I never went back there but, I know he think he got away. One thing I do know is, he got away from me but not from God. God will handle my situation, He might have got away from me but there is someone that's watching at all times. When He punish it be real bad...It come back ten times harder. It might have came back on me, ain't no telling...That's how life goes...

6-22-14

How I feel about me

In real life I love me some me....no matter how hard things get for me or no matter what I have been through, I still love lil ol' me. I love God because he loves me first, I love myself because I keep it so real and just the person I have become is what makes me love me. I love me because I am strong mind, I have a loving heart, I stay in my own lane and mind my own business and I'm smart. I love me even more now because I'm no longer a follower anymore and if I was to follow someone it's going to be someone that's doing something positive in their life. I love me for not killing myself when times got hard and I felt like I wanted to be fucking dead. I love the heart that I have. I love that I love my kids still no matter how hard my baby mommas have made for me. I love my real mom even tho she didn't she didn't keep us when we were young. I love that I like to read the Bible... I love me! I love how God made me, I love the way I look, I love that I don't have to keep looking in the mirror just to love myself, I love the way I act and be funny, I love that I can make my kids smile big, I love that I still love kids even though I have been through a lot dealing with my kids (I still love kids) and the one and only I love and thank God for giving me the heart and mind he gives me to keep on loving the way I do. God Bless! Another thing I love about me is that when someone maybe talking to me and I'll listen to them and what they be saying and the reason for me doing that is because it's rude to not listen and a lot of people love to talk and if they are older then you they may feel like they know more than you and they might know a lot, but that don't mean they know more than you and they might know a lot, but that don't mean they know more than you or smarter than you, so what I'll do is listen and take in everything they say, but all at the same time that don't mean imma do it how you say do it or say it how you say it. Imma still do it my way and you could be right about a lot of what you are saying, but my mind will be telling me don't trust everything someone tell you because they want you to see it how they see it. For some reason my mind won't let me just believe everything someone tell me because I know a lot of people are evil, but I'll listen and be there in the car with you while you talk and put me up game and some of what the person be saying be real and I take that, but not everything. The way I see it people can lead you the wrong way if you let them, so me I let my heart tell me what to do and how to feel. Like I said before I have followed in my younger days, but it was a good reason at the time, but now that I'm older and understand life better, now I lead. You know why? Imma keep it 1000 with me…some people like to talk because they think they know it all, but you listen to them people too because you can learn from them too but use your own mind. They way I look at it is a person that think they know everything you have to listen to them type of people because they love to talk and they wanna be able to point the finger and say I brought that person up right there, so that's why they love to talk and think they know everything. To me sometimes it's cool to listen to the person that don't say to much because you never know what that person is going through, feel or what that person can teach you about yourself and about themselves. My big cousin just wrote me (6-23-14) about using my time wisely because time ain't gone wait on nobody and his reason for writing me this, I really don't know why because I asked him to send me some books to pass time and he send me a lil book about his life. In the book he starts to talk about positive energy and negative energy. I asked for some people magazines or some urban books, now I did tell him I was writing a book on my life, but never told him the name of it or nothing like that just told him what I'm doing and that I'm not just in here (prison) not doing nothing with my time and I did that to see what would be his feedback and his feedback was when you write don't hold nothing back, so I'm like ok that's real, I can do that. I wrote him one more time just letting him know when we use to hang he was like a big cousin but also like a dad to me but more of a cousin. The reason I say cousin more then a dad is because he never pushes me to do positive and all at the same time didn't push me to do negative either but after reading his 7-page book he was talking about how his dad never encourage him, inspired him to do the things he liked to do in life. His dad always would put him down and tell him you aren't that good, so he would believe the shit I guess but all at the same time still do good, but it still affected him. So, whatever it was that he was trying to do he wouldn't take it that far because no one was there to say you can make it or you are doing good. Another thing in the book he was saying that the whole time he was coming up that he wishes that he had a friend like him in his life that wanted money and someone that had the same mind set he had as far as living life. I can say this, then he met me and I know I was on his level that's why he would come get me like all the time to ride with him and not only that I was wishing the same thing out of life was to find a friend that we both had in command and I got that but all at the same time I feel like the both of the people I ended up running with envied me in the back of there mind. It was cool because I knew what I was doing and the plan I had behind it all. My cousin he was the one that could come get me from my grandma house anytime and grandma would let me be with him however long it didn't matter, so it was cool to be with cuz because we would go get girls, go to the mall, go play basketball and he would even let me drive his car. I can't say that he really pushes me to do good in life it's like he just watched me to see what I would do, now he would tell me this or that would happen if I did this or that. Things he would put me up on is how to show love, the kind of books people in prison would read and like I said before girls but anything like going back to school or anything about a career he never really put me up on, now in his book he said that one of his biggest mistakes he made over and over was trying to find a friend who wanted the same thing out of life as he wanted. Someone he could bond with and them both achieve greatness, now I know I came long after he was feeling like this but all at the same time God bless him with that guy he always wanted to bond with and that person was me. Once cuz met me at first, we didn't hit it off, then after a lil time we began to get a lot closer and he started to come by and would let me ride with him, so I really felt like we were close. I didn't really know how he felt in is heart, but all I know is the nigga stayed coming to get me, so I could ride with him. He learned how I was and saw how I was and I was able to see how he was and plus we had each other back, now we both came up different and was not real cousins, but we felt like two real niggas have met and we both always wanted that. I would listen to him because he was the type that like to talk most of the time, so I would sit back and listen, but cuz never really knew how much I knew because he stayed talking all the time (damn!). He just knew I was a cool dude and for some reason we could vibe, so we did. One thing I can remember is one time he had to go to a hotel for this modeling gig and I went with him, but he was picked, and I wasn't. Later I learned I wasn't picked because I was too short, and he was tall, dark skin and bold headed. After we left there I didn't think to much of it, but later learned that modeling didn't go to good for him, so as I got older we stayed talking with each other keeping in contact and that's when he was putting me up on acting and telling me all the money I could make. I would listen and all at the same time be thinking like damn I do need to be doing something positive because I am getting older. I took all the steps, so I could start the acting. I just still went my own way by doing the modeling first, that's just to get my face out there, then take a lil acting classes so I could see how that go and how they do things with acting. All at the same time cuz never said back in the days aye cuz let's go do acting and see if we could blow, because I know, and he know I would have done it, but he wanted to do it by himself and that shit didn't work out. Later, in life he put me up on it, so I could try it because he knew if he got in my head about how much money was being made doing it I would try it and I did go for it. When I started it he had something to say about that, and it was I need to act and I'm like cuz I got this I'm doing it and he only complimented me on one picture out of all the pictures I ever took...it's cool though, he just make me feel like every sense I started the modeling/acting it seem like to me cuz really isn't happy for me and not only that every time I start something he bring up another ideal but the ideals he bring up be cool but he never go through with them. He put them off on me to see if ill do it and if it's involving money ill try it but he only come up with the ideal and put it off on me...now with the acting I know my cousin wanted to be a part of that but like he say so many people was in his head saying boy you better get a job and you can't do this and that and that took a toll on him, so he never made in the acting because he stop. So, what he did was put in my head how much money people made and got me into it. I'm thinking he wanted me to live his dream because he didn't have the right mind set to do it, so he put it off on the next best person and that was me and I went for it. When he seen that I started I don't ever remember my big cousin saying aye cuz I see you doing good on the pictures you been taking. He just told me he liked this one photo of me and I never understood why he liked that photo out of all the photo's I have took. I know he know how much that would have meant to me by him out all people tell me I'm doing good keep up the good work. Just because he was missing that from his dad. Don't let that what your dad does to you do to someone else. Be better than your dad and when you find a lil dude you take a liking to, be there for him, show him things and tell him things that will make him smile and feel good about himself. That's what count...he tells me when I start losing friends and all the things he was telling me was happing but all at the same time I still felt like I also was losing him in a way that he might have thought I could deal with it. Cuz always told me I was smarter then I think, so when I go around my homeboy I really can't say I followed him the whole time but, in some ways, I did but what I was doing was watching him do things because like I say he was from town and I was from the country. The city was a lot faster so being around him I felt like I needed to watch him do things before I did things, I can't say I watch him and some of him rubbed off on me like getting money, liking nice things and looking fly. He was good at those things so that's why we could kick it so hard and he was drug free and I was too. To me I was just doing the things he liked to do so I could learn some things but like I say he ended up going to prison and it left me in the streets all by myself in the game. I did pretty good in the streets while my homeboy was gone but for some reason I still felt like I needed him, but he wasn't there, so I linked up with some lil homie from our same hood and started viben with them and that's when I started thuggin, popping pills and smoking weed. I can't say it all was a bad thing because the weed was making me see things I never notice before. The pills made me real horny and loveable. I loved every bit of that but being that people around my city never knew I did drugs they felt like I was going crazy, but I wasn't going crazy I was living life. As time went on I started to lose money, spending a lot on getting high when my street money had done slowed down but I still wanted to get high and I did. After experiencing bad pills at times made me want to stop using and after being on probation for such a long of a time made me want to stop smoking weed, even though I V.O.P one time for smoking weed I still was coming to an end about getting high and I was getting into working out all at the same time…getting high don't mix with working out but now I'm in prison, no smoking, still working out, but before I came to prison I would get up with my homeboy because by this time he was out of prison before I went and he felt like I was crazy for doing drugs but not to me. I told him X makes the sex better, I never told him about weed but he seen me smoke before but that weed be letting you know. My homie really didn't want to be around me because I started thuggin but what I think it is he just mad I wasn't still on the same shit he was on and that's doing nothing and the way I see it is if we was real friends don't fucking judge me or try to look down on me because anything you can do I can do better…I was still dressing and still hitting the gym. I just wasn't making a lot of street money like we did before. My phone had slowed down and not only that I was older and a lot wiser. I wasn't going back to look for the money like thugging was legal...shiiit these crackas will hide ya ass, so I had to fall back but now I'm in prison for V.O.P., but now wipping up something a whole lot better.

    My youngest brother Flex, me and him was the one that live with grandma and when we got there I don't what was going on with him, but he was really a bad ass. Some type of way he was back home before me and when I would get home from school to go in our room he would have done fucked up the whole room for no reason, I mean the beds, curtain's everything was messed up and I just never understood why he would get home and do these things and this would be for some time that he did these things. I asked grandma can I have my own room because lil brah was doing way too much and I had to be the one to clean everything up after he done messed it all up. After some time with living with grandma lil brah started to live with grandma daughter. She was nice at times, but she had her lazy ways and being that lil brah was staying with her he was her go do it "guy." Go do this, Flex pick this up for me, will you clean this up for me and this list just keep on going and to keep it real I really didn't like that my lil brother had to live with her and be her maid around her house but hey I was still young and couldn't do nothing about anything, so I just fell back. She was my/our foster sister but like I say her fat ass was lazy and being that lil brah was there he was doing a lot. Lil brah was bad though, I mean he done been locked up for whatever reason and being that he no longer lived with me and our older brother at grandma house we didn't know what was really going on. I found out later that my sister ended up getting a boyfriend that went to school with me and do you know me, and dude use to hang back in the days but as we got older he ended up getting my sister and after he moved in with her they ended up having a baby. Dude started to use coke cain and me not knowing and maybe our sister not knowing my lil brah later told me that dude was the one that asked him to try this drug, that's how lil brah told me that's how he started to use coke cain. It made me mad when lil brah told me that because he was still a lil kid when dude brought this life to him. After lil brah went to prison for two years he got out and told me he doesn't do it no more. After being out for no more then a year he ended up getting 15 years for the same thing that got him in prison the first time and that was stealing people shit.

6.29.14

Thinking in Prison

Feelings

Sometimes I might get or be in my feelings, but not too much. I try to stay away from getting in my feelings because I'm trying to complete a mission. I try to stay away from feelings even though there is nothing wrong with showing feelings; I just try to stay away from them. Being in prison can play with your mind, heart and make you feel some type of way. If you feel like someone ain't there for you like they said they will be or would be or if your not getting the love you feel like you need or want. It can make your feel like you are alone or even down, but like I say Jesus is always with us no matter what. One thing I do know is my baby momma want to play with me, being that I have love for her like I do I still feel like she wants to see me hurt rather than see me happy. The reason I say that is because like I say, "When I first got here (prison) she would write me all the time, talking about she feel bad and sad that I'm here. I will tell her I'm good everything is going to be okay as long as she be here with me while I do this time. Now me being me I never put all trust in nobody I put all trust in Jesus, that was my back up plan. I act some what like I believe what she was saying, but being that I know her and being around her all of this long time and not only I been around her, I became her friend so I can know her better than she think. When she tried the bullshit I'll see it coming and know how to chill and not get in my feelings. Deep down that's what she want me to do because she wants control and see me down. How I know is because I know my friend. I know you're thinking or saying to yourself how or why you still feeling this woman if you know all these things about her. Let me tell you when we would be by our selves with no kids she was and would be so cool, we would hang out, have good sex on pills (x-pill). She listens to me because I love to talk so we got to know each other very well and I never fell in love, but doing these things made me have mad love for the young lady. While we was having our good times at first we had our ups and downs because I feel like her mom was in the picture, in her ear trying to make her feel some type of way about me. Once moms was out the picture we was chill, now baby momma would say the reason she ain't so called feeling me because I'll put my hands on her. I'm not even going to lie I would give her a blow to the stomach if she got me wrong or she tried to play head games with me and the kids. Some people might say that it's wrong, but I think it's wrong to play with kids and their dad making the kids feel some type of way about their dad or taking the kids to your mom house just to keep the kids away from their dad because yall are not getting alone because you want the kids to take your side. So you take the kids somewhere you don't even want to be just to make the dad mad (so me being me, bitch I would hurt you for doing something like that to me and my kids) that's why we would get into it. Baby momma would write me and tell me she want a man that's not going to put his hands on her, but what she want is a fuckin duck azz nigga that's going to let her do what the fuck she want (not me). I'm not the one! I'm not going to put my hands on her because I'm crazy or because I get drunk and want to fight (hell no). I want to punch her in her shit because she want tot play head games and it's dealing with our kids and I know our kids need me to be there. So if you want play games you might get punched in ya shit, but if you act like a mom or a real mother you will get treated like a Queen. I love her because the time we have shared and we have three kids that would want both of their parents there, but like I say women will have kids from you and find a reason to want to depart. Especially, if you don't have the money you use to have shhit there going to try you in ways they said they would never do. As long as your cash is right they would ride, fight and have as many kids in the world you want; they want leave for shit. Yall can fight anytime shhit most of the time she gone start the fight (money talk I'm telling ya). When there is no money like that coming in a woman would find everything wrong with your azz, you ain't no good, she want more than a friendship, I wasn't ready so now she's not ready, I like to put my hands on her and she's not with that. I mean the list goes on and on. They are only happy when you are a "boss" that's it. For me (Men) don't fall on your dick because your woman is going to start acting up. I know a lot of women out there are saying a real woman is not like that it should be about loving the person you're with, but yall women know this nigga need to be ridin in a Bentley to keep getting that pussy. If he don't got the cash he aint gone get that azz, now it is women that is real and not looking at if the nigga is paid or not because if he is a good man then he's going to know how love her the way she wants to be loved. So if dude don't have the money it's cool with her because she is getting the next best thing and that's love. She already know with money comes a lot of other women, fighting for him and all, so to each it's on. As time went on and me being with baby momma (2) and me knowing how she wanted to play head games with me an the kids it made me back away from my kids in a way because I didn't want to be hurt, my feelings being played with or even them getting miss treated because they are acting like they are having fun with their dad and not their mom lol. I know its crazy right, that's how it's been with me so far. What I would do and still do is love them in my heart, but in font of their mom act like I'm not feeling them (my kids) that much. That way me and the kids would be giving their mom all the attention so she want think nothing and get mad and we (the kids) would still get love from her all at the same time. I know it's carzy ☺! I wanted to be around and I still wanted to be around my friend…one thing I do and did know is my kids did and do love me and they seen what was going on. At the time I was still living with my baby momma #2 so I was around the kids too, but the one child I really had a bond with was my 2nd oldest because I had him in the midst of having my own and having money so baby momma had to fall back because I was the boss and she was feelin it and she didn't mind her/our son being around his dad so chilled out. Now all at the same time I/we had our son baby momma seen I had the hood fuckin with me, niggas wanted to be around me and I had money and could buy what I wanted…Our baby boy was really fucked up about me like he was I know a sense of jealously came over her, but I didn't know at the same time because we was just livin life. As time went on I discovered these things, I'm good at paying attention at things…so after our son was took and went to stay with her mom that was her escape to try to get closer to our son, but my son wasn't having it; he wanted me. The sad thing about it was I was young and stuck in my ways till I didn't do what it took at the time to get him back. I did visit him, but that stopped after awhile, so while he (our son) was with baby momma mom me and baby momma still could be around each other and I would cry to her because I knew my heart and our son heart was hurting. I know her wanted to be with me/us…so I use to cry my heart out to baby momma and all we do is get on x-pills, spend time together and fuck all the time, but my pain for my son never went away. I just pop because the sex was great and me and baby momma was becoming very cool, because she was like my best friend/lover, but we still had our ups and downs and I knew she still had something up her sleeve. She would put her lil plan to the side and vibe hard with me so I thought she was real but she wasn't! She was becoming more and more like her mom everyday. Then she would get cool and we would have sex and be back cool. In the midst of us being cool we had another lil boy and lil girl and I discovered she wanted them to be fucked up about her like our first son is fucked up about me, so what she did was with our lil boy (2nd) she stayed doing everything for him making our son feel like she was the only parent and I was just the little helper. She would change him and cook for her and the boys to make them feel some type of way to turn them against me (it was working) till I would put my foot down to let my other son know I was his daddy and I would be there for him too, but our 2nd son still took more liking to his mom then me…Our first son would say this is my dad and to his brother this is your mom. We were divided like fuck in the same house, then she would put that pussy on me then we had a lil girl. Oh boi you already know what happened then…like I say I was there when all the kids came out and I was there for my/our lil girl. After I signed the papers at the hospital and we left shit still got bad we would still get into it and I was scared to get close to our lil girl because I didn't want to get played with. While we would be at baby momma house I would never really pick up our lil girl or show any love because I was scared. Now at the hospital I was showing love holding her taking pictures with her, but when we got home I just stopped! After seven days of our lil girl being born and home with us I was put in jail for domestic violence. Her mom called the police over to her apartment because baby momma was on the phone with her sister and baby momma wanted me to leave and I wouldn't so I got up to pick up my lil girl and baby momma ran out the door and started crying and got on the phone and called her sister and her sister called their mom and the mom called the police over to the apartment. Baby momma did tell me I needed to leave, but me being a hard azz I said no! Not because I just didn't want to but because I didn't want to leave my kids and my lil girl. I took my lil girl in the room I looked out the window and saw the police and I'm like you called the police on me so I go back in the room, come back out as the police was coming in the house and was like damn you called the police on me for real while touching baby momma shoulder and front of the police. So the police took me to jail for touch or strike. Now, mind you baby momma mom already had my baby mom to put out an adjunction on me already, so I wasn't really suppose to be over her house. I was still there, so now I was going to jail in front of my kid and our oldest was "crying" about to run to the police car, but baby momma sister stopped him…I was mad as fuck about the shit! I couldn't do shit! I get to the jail and get booked in and they tell me I couldn't call baby momma or have any contact with her…shhit and soon as I got to the phone I called baby momma/friend and we would talk and talk. Until, one day I was on the phone with her and she was going to pick up our kids, but she seen the police at the daycare for some reason as she was pulling up. I'm telling her you straight they ain't there for you, after we get off the phone I called back later to find out they was there for our kids. They took our kids and put them all at baby momma moms house, boi was baby momma mad. The jail had recorded us on the phone like "87 times" talking, so being that they see we wasn't going to stop talking they took our kids and it's not like I didn't know I couldn't talk to baby momma, I still felt like I wanted to talk to my "friend" and I did! Not knowing what they was going to do to us, but talking our kids I didn't know that was one of them, but they did. So, I knew baby momma really ain't want to harm me deep in her heart, I know her mom was in her head bad and being that she wanted love from her mom she listened to her about the things to do to me….so after being in jail for some time I end up going to court on the domestic violence charge and pleading guilty and they gave me 10 months probation. I get out and hit baby momma up the next day and she come see me and we hit it back. She was there for me the whole 10 months to help me get off probation. In the mist of her trying to please me she was also trying to please her mom. Her mom was still treating her bad, but her mom had her kids so baby momma would do what she had to do even if it was to leave me. I felt alone because baby momma was doing too much if you ask me just to please this lady. This lady would call my baby momma off her job to change our second oldest son or bathe him, like what the fuck! This bitch was crazy, so me and baby would get into it because she couldn't leave her mom house without her mom telling her let your brother ride with you, it was a lot. I couldn't be around my kids too much or be around my kids at all until I finished my case plan…which I did! "Boi" it was a lot! But it got done, thank God! I can say this girl wanted love from her mom and still didn't get it and at the same time turned on me the one that was there to help her get through the bullshit her mom and sister was taking her through…I'm still around we still ended up getting our kids back and I still ended up living in the same house with baby momma and the kids. Being there sometimes still got crazy, but I didn't leave. In my heart I "wanted" too because I got tired of the bullshit with her ungrateful ass, but still in my heart I wanted to stay (until I had to come to prison). Now she want to be by herself lol so she put my stuff in storage so when I get out I won't be at her place lol, but she still would write me and say the kids miss you (we miss you), but won't come see me lol. Shit Crazy! I still really don't know how to feel about anything, ya feel me! I still love her and the kids, but I feel like and know she want me to feel down, but that's not going to happen. When they release me and I get to this money I'm going to show her how a boss do his 1, 2...now do I think she love me, oh yeah! She also hate on me and wanted to be better than me lol, you know what it ain't happening. She might as well join me or be against me, however she want to play it I'm down for it. She let the kids send me a Father's Day card with all their names in it and hers, after that she hasn't wrote me yet...as far as my little girl she know daddy, but they (baby momma) be trying her hardest to keep me and my lil girl away. While I was staying with my baby momma and the kids and I see the bullshit baby momma be pullin trying to have our lil girl go everywhere she go or make our lil girl feel some type of way, if our lil girl don't follow her around the house. Baby momma just wanted this lil girl up her ass and it's funny to me because I get to see what a person would do just to feel or be loved. My thing is I'm her dad and she needs me, but like I say when I get tired of the bullshit and put my foot down and cause hell in the house and make my lil girl seat down with me and her brothers and watch TV and tell her we ya family too. Baby momma feel like sense it's a girl they need to vibe more and let the boys vibe with me, no let them kids be kids and be wherever they want to be in the house. As long as they ain't killing each other or trying to go outside on their own it's fine. They have two parents and they suppose to love the both of us...I sent a picture home to my kids and one for my mom and my baby momma wrote me telling me the kids was happy see my to picture and was fighting over whose going to hold the picture, so that made me feel good. She put in the letter my lil girl I seen the picture and was like daddy! I know she love me...everybody want to love on my kids, but they want the kids to stay away from me and when they do that and I be around other kids them kids love me like crazy. I come to realize when people are unhappy with their situation they would try their hardest to bring the next person down, not because they don't love that person. They just don't know no better and they be mad because the person that is not going through it in their eyes, so the one that is going through it want to make he/she feel pain because they feel pain...

7.1.14

My Workout

Me working out in prison is all I pretty much do, it helps past time and keep my mind off things that will probably try to make me stress. What I'll do is occupy my mind and body to stay away from the bull… what I do is put my mind on the prize and the prize is me making a lot of money when I get out of prison. While I been here one of the most things I have ran into is a lot of books and some of them be urban or fitness, but I really been into lately is the fitness books because you can make money for working out and having a nice ripped up body. All we do here is workout so I been going hard, I want to see if I can get a gold medal around my kids neck…see the way I see it is I'm not just working out for nothing like just staying in good shape. I'm working out to hopefully one day get paid for my body and I really don't care what it is for me to get paid. Right now I'm already in modeling/acting I want to do fitness maybe even porn shhit it don't matter shhit I don't have no girlfriend so really to me I can just live my life and get paid for fucking beautiful women. It's really for the money and to really make some people mad because they can't do it or don't have the heart to do it. The way I look at the porn thing is I'll also be doing it for fun also to bring something new to the game of having sex; I have a nice body, handsome, cute, and funny! Now I know there will be some women out there will say they can make me nut fast and shit like that but let me tell you this you have another thing coming if you think if I'm going to let you do that. We will be getting paid to have sex so that mean we need to make it fun and we need to have lots of fun so no commin quick besides, the ladies. I also want to do a clothing line, but there is one thing that I need and that's the money to start it off…I'm going to try going to school and after getting my books with the money they give me for school, I'm going to look into doing t-shirts for men and women and see how much money I can bring in. Then I'll start a website so people can go on to see what I'm doing as far as my shirts and maybe someone will come alone with more ideas to help me grow. My reason for going so hard in a lot of these things, I'm trying to do is because I have four kids, but only three I get to see and spend time with. I want to give them the good life, I want them to see daddy with the big house, nice car and have them with a lot of money in the bank all four of them (that's my goal). Last is to stay out of jail or prison so I'll be able to go to every game they have unless daddy is working. When I was making street money I did get to see my oldest son. My thing was to keep him dress at all times, have him with nice shoes and clothes and a nice gold set around his neck and wrist…back then I never thought about putting money in the bank for him or even saving, I was living for right then. I can say I spend a lot of money on him and it made me feel good just to do that. Only if my son was old enough to remember over half the things we did get to do, he would just smile ☺. I use to go in for him and be there for him no matter what…fuck child support, I didn't need the white folks to make me take care of my son, that was my mean ass hateful baby momma doin just to make me and my son life hard. I liked to see my son clean with his hair done looking just like me, then on top of all of that I had a nice car for him to ride in. In the end my son and all the things I brought was taken from me… now I have to see how I can get all of these things back again including my son. Before he come back I want to be paid like I was before, so when he/they stop by and want to see their dad they're not going to want to leave my house or me and their going to have a fat bank account put up for them. I want to be someone my kids can look up to and be able to say my dad has this, my dad has a nice car and my dad has a nice house…to me its pay back for all the times I've missed in their life. Get money by any means!

The Things I Use to Care about I Don't Care About Anymore

I use to care about a lot, but being that I have seen and been through so much I really don't care about a lot of things no more. To me it's helpful because it helps me to control my feelings and stay away from being or getting so angry when someone wants to try to push your button… I want to live in peace as much as I can because it helps me be more joyful and I love how I can be when I am at peace…The way I look at it is once you have seen it or been their most of the time it's hard for it too really bother you like that again. It's like you can see bullshit before it gets to you! If you can see it, why let it make you mad or upset? There will be time I might want to get mad or be upset but I feel like it's not going to help any. All it's going to do is make me madder and then I'll think about some crazy shit that I need to stay away from or keep my mind off of. Having a clear mind help you think better, it keeps you happy, you can make others happy and you just go on and on a little stress free. Now I can say I won't never get stress about anything because I am human and I do have a heart. That means I still have feelins' but all at the same time the things that use to make me mad, I'm not going to let it make me mad anymore; doing that have gotten me in a lot of trouble or in bad situations, so now I'm going to chill and play it another way. I know it can be more peaceful staying away from angry, being mad and having an attitude on every corner about everything. I have too do better with myself...Job 6:1-3 I wish my great pain could be weighed! I wish all of my sufferings could be weighed on scales! I'm sure they would weigh more than the grains of sand on the sea shore.

7.2.14

Thinking in Prison

Sitting here thinking about my kids...the things they would say to me when I was home with them like, "Dad I like your shoes," lol that's my four year old Bad Azz, my Fats he want to be just like me, if not better than me lol. The first photo shoot I put him in took him to a whole another level because, now when he get fresh he can turn his swag on and be so cool. It's just so funny to see him turn up like he do. Bad Azz he is a nice lil dude with a very nice smile, very respectful, but all at the same time can be a bad azz for real. Lil dude can have a very bad attitude lol. I know he get that from me and his mom. The reason he even get the name Bad Azz is because when Bad Azz was in the womb lil dude was very active. He just seemed like he was going to be a bad azz, so what I did was named my son Bad Azz. Last, My lil girl lol she is something else, when she really didn't walk that much she was so precious. When she was took and came back around me it's like they had did something to my lil girl. She was stubborn as hell and trying to be mean like her mom, and I was not having that at all. I want her to be better than her mom, not some girl around here that don't know nothing with a stank attitude that want to have her way. At first when we got back around each other me and her didn't get alone, but before I left and came to prison me and her became pretty cool. I think it was she was use to getting her way with all the other people she was around, when it came to daddy and daddy would make her do this or sit down, she didn't know anything about that part of her life so I had to give it to her the hard way lol. I know she's going to respect me for it later on in life and we love each other…I love them all!

7-5-14

Nigga's really act like gay ass bitches…everywhere. I go once I get to a dorm and get settled in and get right so I can start my workout. Now me! I really don't need one to workout with. I'm going to get it done anyway but sometimes you'll run into someone that want to so call workout with you. One thing about me is I pay attention to everything and not only that being in prison makes it worse because I'm around a lot of thieves and convicts so I'm very on alert because you never know what these dudes be on or what be on there mind. I must be on guard always. I'm a dude and I'm around a lot of dudes and I don't know if it's me or my mind is fucked up, but a lot of these dudes is gay, and I don't mean happy or have gays ass way. I have seen or ran into dudes seem like they are straight, and they be cool, but the gay dudes aren't cool. The reason I say that is because they undercover gays and they want you to be on what they on since we in prison. Not fuckin me nigga, I'm a real nigga and I love women but my reason for venting about this gay shit is because I'm around it all the fucking time. I don't have a problem with the gay dudes that you know are gay it's the ones that are undercover that fuck with me and how I know they be gay or have gay ass ways is because at first when they first talk to you they try to be or stay cool but really they trying to feel you out and I don't know if I have a look that say come try me or what on my face but they ease my way to see. I might look like a nice guy or a quit dude that stay to myself but that's not really the case. I stay to myself because I don't have time for the gay shit or fuck shit, so I stay to myself, now if you feel like you "G"ed up and want to talk then we can chop it up and that's how some of the dudes will come at me, like they so "G"ed up so they can see what I be bout and be on and when I open my mouth I give them "G" shit all the way. The whole time I'm talking to them I'm watching there every movement and I listen to them talk too, and a lot of times I do more listing then talk because I know when I start to talk the shit be so real till it push niggas away so I mostly sit back and listen and how I feel them out is to see if they can take a liken to me to see if I'm cool like I look so they start their conversation off talking about women to wheel me in, then this one dude started to like hit me on the sly, then I sit in a spot to where he can't touch me, then what he started to do is when I be up on my bunk he'll come get me up and start talking about something then want to touch till I told him aye stop touching while you talk because he was getting to the point where he hitting on the leg, he was doing too much then on the top of that I learned by watching him he have girl ways but he talk about all these girls he done had in the past so I listen but when I listen to him he tell me how he use to always be with his momma and a dude like me be feeling like if you was raised by your mom 9 times out of ten you have bitch ways and he do. These dudes are a trip tho. They be having girlfriends out on the streets but when they get locked up with dudes you see another side to them. I love women and being in prison make me want a woman even more, but my only thing is I'm going to just try to make better choices when picking them. Shiiiit I tried that this time and last time and these pussy hoes be on some bullshit lol but it's all good I still love'em but you best believe when I get back right it's going to be pay back fa sho! To all the ladies watch out for these dudes that want to be a thug or pretty boy wanna be because that nigga might want more dick then you ever had then your ass gone be sitting up there talking about T Dog told me to watch out for bitch niggas like you and ya ass gay sitting up here fucking me, but you really want a dude. Ladies watch his walk.

7.9.14

Ma, this one for you…I understand how you came up and being on drugs…ain't nobody perfect…I'm happy to thank you for still having all your kids and not having a abortion after being on drugs and always having to fight with daddy. I just feel like the things you have done to me and for me are cool cause I don't hate you for it. I can say all the times you tried to make me feel jealous when I brought people in your life that you took a liking to, you wanting to be rude about my kids saying your kids, when my kids is not your fuckin kids, they are your grandkids and don't you ever forget that. I'm the reason why you even know my kids anyway. You can't act like they are your kids when you have kids of your own that you barely want to help out in life, think you are going to forget about your own kids and take care or help take care of my kids…it don't work like that with me. I brought my kids in your life so you could be a grandparent to them not a fuckin mom sorry! I know it was times when I asked you to be there for me and you never showed up, you have lied to me in my face about things you have took from me, your fuckin attitude is bad as hell, make me not ever really want to be around you that much. Yea, you can be cool at times but, all at the same time the things I have seen you do in my face make me want to hate yo ass but, the heart that I have want let me. I know you have a drug problem and you being using for a long time and that's cool but, my thing is…in real life I/we need and needed you more than you can dream of…Do unto others as you would want them to do unto you and that goes for any and everybody…the things you have done to me, the reason why I know you did them is because of your drug use and the lack of respect you have for me as your son. You wasn't the one who raised me, the only way you started to have respect for me is when I was doing good and not staying with you and your boyfriend. That's when I had money…when I came to town from the country and people would see me they would say to me, "You look like one of them and I would smile, then they would say, "I hope you are nothing like them at all" and I would say, "I'm not, there are just my people." Some people say good things about my family, then you have the ones that keep it real and tell me not to be like them "my family." Me and all my brothers are in prison, are you here for us? Do you send us money every month? Yes, you have sent me cards for my birthday and I thank you for that, yes you may be out there with my kids doing this or that for them but, what about your own kids, we have feelings too… "But ima keep it G"…I come around you and bring my kids because my brothers don't care to be around you like that. It's not like I care to much either but, I do it because we/I am your child. We want you to have our back and be there for us but, you rather take liking to someone else. I still come around and show you whatever you try to do to me to make me feel jealous it really ain't going to work because I know I am a good son and the things you don't do for me and my brothers, I'll do them for my brothers and ask God to help me do them. God been holding us all down the whole time we been away from you and when we come back to you, you don't even give us the right love; shhit you rather talk about us or steal from me and blame someone else…the table do turn. I still love you though I just want you to hear and understand my pain, ain't nothing like that mother and father love and since we was in foster homes and now we can vibe with you we want love that's all.

7.10.14

Thinking in Prison

Today been pretty cool for me. It's started out like kind of rough because I felt kind of sick because I be getting these boil ups on my body for some reason. It had my sick a lil bit this morning but, after taking Ibuprofen I feel a lot better…I hate being sick because it stops you from things you like to do to pass time and my thing is I like to work out to pass time. The way I felt this am I really did want to workout but, once I got off work and we had to go to the rec yard I was able to do some pull ups. After that I went and laid down for a few then woke back up and was able to do a lot of push ups and other work outs. I still could not do my abs because my butt check hurt on the one side, so I couldn't lay on my back to do abs. I tried but it was hurting too bad so I stopped, I was mad too. I had mad energy to do a whole lot so since I couldn't do my abs I went even harder on my other workouts till this dude that sleeps beside me woke up and was like, "aye that workout is really cutting you up!" I'm like, "Yeah! ☺" So I smiled and said, "I'm glad you told me because now I'm going to go harder." Being that I don't look in the mirror I can't and don't see my body that much to see what I look like and the reason for that is because I want to keep working and one day look in the mirror and surprise myself. See after I work out I already feel good so to me there is no reason to look in the mirror, I just really thank God for giving me the energy to be able to go hard like I do. Besides, I'm not into myself like that too stay in the fuckin mirror. Some of these dudes in here stay in the mirror like they are a beauty queen or something…Like I say ain't nothing wrong with it it's just not for T Dog! I leave the looking for the ladies to do I already know I'm on point anyways because I go hard and I have these niggas in here trying to keep up. Not only that they stay with their eyes on a nigga lol all I do is smile a shake my head and say, "Yeah! Lol I'm getting right." I told myself I want to be in a fitness books and that's my goal and I'm going to do it if the Lord let me… "Strong mind, strong body!" The one thing that gets me is these dudes in here get mad because a nigga go so hard when a nigga work out lol and it's crazy to me because they can do the same thing but, I guess they ass can't. So I guess while they be looking at me all crazy and shit lol. Another thing I put in my head while I workout is people on the outs that think I might have fell off, got me fucked up! I'm still swagged the fucked up with a nice azz body…I'm not going to let nothing stop what I'm trying to do in life and I know anybody can say what won't stop them while they are locked up but, me T Dog I do it for my kids and for anybody that thought I fell off. I might not have the money I use to have but the good thing is I'll make more than I use to make and still thug in my own lil way… just for the ladies! They say, "Mo money, mo problems." Well bring on the problems because when I get this fuckin paper I'm going to do some real shit and one is going to be to get me a Bentley (Big Dreams). I never try to be finer than the ladies no, that's not me! I just keep my body in good shape for my health and for the ladies out there that want a man in their life that have a great body, that ain't scared or lazy to work out and yes, of course I have to stay in good shape so the sex game can be crazy! The women these days want a man that have a strong back and beat their back out if it came to that, you feel me? You don't always have to have the biggest but if you can work it with that strong back, you in there like swim wear... It's dudes in prison that want to be finer than the fuckin women and when they walk you can see the bitch in them (in that fuckin walk). The nigga is fuckin gay! I'm seeing it now how some of these dudes is, walk like a fuckin bitch and get mad because you ain't on that gay shit with them (undercover is what you call it).

7.11.14

Thinking in Prison

I'm sitting here thinking to myself about what it's going to be like when I leave prison...yes I do have plans, but I really don't have a place to stay. All my so called friends are on some other shit than what I'm on and in order to try and get something from them, I'm thinking I'm going to have to act like I'm in the streets real heavy. Which, I don't mind doing shhit I'm trying to get back on my feet, but still not trying to go back to the streets. Niggas don't want to hear you say, "You want to do a clothing line or you want to go to go to school." These niggas want to hear you say you back in these streets head first. I do and I am going to see if I can get into school and take up some classes...I'm not trying to move back with my mom and baby momma ain't fuckin with me so I'm kind of fucked up right now...I still have faith that's something is going to come through for me, I ain't losing hope, it's just something I think about how it is going to be for me; with me getting out to nothing and no one. I guess I'm going to have to find the ladies, but what I really need is a job; so I can pay this back child support and get my DL's back until then I will not be driving shhit! Want get me back in here prison for driving. I did get this dude number before I left the county jail and he said he will get me a job so I'm going to try him out. I have a brother that's out of prison and I see he hasn't hit me up while I been here shhit like I say, he stopped by our mom house looking for me but, momma told him, "I was here" and all he told her is to tell me to "stay out of trouble and I'll be okay." What I needed him to do was shoot momma his address or something so I could hit him up but no address, no brah didn't hit me up and in a way it make me feel some type of way. I feel like the nigga only wanted to holla at me to see if I was still in the streets to try to come up…but damn nigga when is one of my brothers going to be there to help me come up is what I keep asking myself. It's like all of us have our life but, everybody want to find me when it's time to come up. See when my brother that just got out went to prison I already knew he wasn't going to be writing me that much. It's not because I wouldn't write back or because I was mad about anything but, I knew he wasn't going to be writing me like that because he did grow up around his other brothers. I knew he had other family on his daddy side that he would be keeping in contact with besides his brothers on his mom side (that was the case). He did write me one time and I hit him back but, after I hit him back he never wrote me again don't know why; he just never did. He did talk with him while he was at work release and over FaceBook once and one of the main things he asked me was, "I still in the streets," I told him, "No!" Not just no to say no, no for #1 we are over this computer and in real life I'm not in the streets like that anymore. Still in my head I'm saying to myself, "This nigga want me to help him come up."

7.13.14

Thinkin In Prison

Summertime, in prison at work so called chillin…thinkin to myself about how I don't want to come back, I'm also thinking about all the time them folks up there in the courthouse is giving out. The one dude that tried to rob me I just seen him in the newspaper, they just gave him life and that's not for all of his charges. That shit is fuckin with me like I almost got the time...but all it is I'm tired of this place and I don't want to come back. My 24 months is long enough, I want to get out and make a lot of money somehow. So, I can have my own and my kids will have a nice place to come to so they can see me. Being around these undercover gay ass niggas just makes me sick...all I'm going to say is I'm going to do my best to get a job, but if that don't work I'm going to what I know best. Shhhh it's not drugs...I know one thing I put in my head is I really don't have to worry about my kids when I get out as far as rushing to take care of them when they are being well taking care of right now. Daddy come home I don't have to put in my head I need to hurry and get in these streets to get this money so I can take care of my kids, shhit if they getting token care of now then they will when I get out too. All they want to do is see Daddy so we can play and get all my lil hugs from all of them☺. I damn sho' ain't going to get out and run the streets so I can come back here. You will catch me in the gym staying rocked up, looking slim and sexy...seeing dude in the paper fucked my head up, shhit these people are giving out real time with one fuck up and ya ass is gone. I been thinking about my lil brother a lot because he is doing 15 years right now and now that I'm in prison I really know what it's like to be here in prison, with no visits, no one to call, no one to really write and the one that he could write is now locked up and that's me! I feel his pain, when I get my money right I'll make sure I shoot him a lawyer first so he can give some of that back. Then I will shoot him some money to put on his books and some pictures...now I really know what it's like to not have and not only that I love my lil brah, shhit look what we done been through that could be a part of why lil brah was thuggin like he was. I don't care what he did and if I don't be there for him nobody else will. I can bet nobody is even thinking about my brother...when Plies said, "Motherfuckers forget about you when your bid long that shit is so fuckin TRU!" Right now one of the things that's been bothering me is, is I didn't have the adjunctions on me I would be gone to work release by now. The prison won't let you go to work release if you have a violent charge or any type of adjunctions...so I'm fuckin stuck here in prison til my EOS date. When I first got here I was saying it's cool if I didn't go to work release that way when I leave here I'll be going straight home, but shhit after being here for some time, boiii you want to "go" somewhere, shhit at work release at least you'll be a lil free plus get a job. It's better than being here you'll whole time. At then center you can see your family and get some pussy (RIGHT NOW MY DICK IS BEGGING FOR SOME PUSSY). I was sleep yesterday, but not in a deep sleep, next thing I know my mind had me thinking about some girl I was on top of. All I was doing in the dream with her was rubbing my nut sack on her pussy and I guess you know what came next. In my head I was saying it wasn't real but my mind and dick was feeling the lil dream FUCK!!!…I want to go to work release! I thought in my in my mind it would be cool to do all my time here, but fuck that I want to go to work release (I'm tired of being here).

7-15-14

Never Give Up

No matter what I have been through I won't let it hold me back from being more positive in life or stop me from teaching my kids I come across the right way of life. I know that's what I feel like I was missing is someone that not only be there for me but also teach me and point me in the right path. Not just be around me because I can pull hoes! If you get into it with some people/niggas you know I'll back, you or even jump in the fight and that's if your winning or not. Point me down the right path if you got love for me. Show me you really care by putting me up on things in life that's going to help me in the long run so when I get older I can look back and say boi I'm glad you were in my life to show me the way. By not pointing someone in the right path while they are young they will pay for it when they get older. If you teach them good in life it will stick with them and they'll be a lot happier with what you have done verses the other bullshit. If you teach bullshit bullshit is all they'll know til they get older and find out that bullshit is not going to get you nowhere in life but prison if not left behind. One thing I can say is it's never to late to find the right path. Some people you teach bullshit that shit will stick with them and they never shack it and they in up pushin the same bullshit off on someone else or someone they love not really because they want to but because that's all they were taught. Not having both parents there will take a big toll on kids also or just having one parent there can affect a child also because some kids be feeling like they are missing one or the other so that give them reason to act out. Life is crazy and for some of us it is design to be crazy for us. The good part about that is God be with us the whole time til we find a way for ourselves, so what im telling you no matter what never stop trying and if your going to be in someone life that you have love for show them real love and don't hold back. One thing I know is sometime people you might be around will be on bullshit and it could be your friend, brother, sister, or cousin. They might be on the bullshit because they know you'll follow them or even help them. That's why I say you must be a leader because if you don't you gone fall in some bullshit and bullshit is not what you want. The same person that's on the bullshit could be just doing it so you can help them. In the long run when they get what they want and you have nothing they gone leave ya azz. Some people have snake ways and is out for themselves. If you don't have your own mind or a snake way behind what ya'll have going on you could be running into a dead end. Always think ahead always! Now if you have a real friend and ya'll on some bullshit together keep it real with him no matter what but trust no man no matter what! Stay ahead of the game the game! The way I see it is some people you be around might be for you and then you have the ones that's mad because they aren't you. They be ready to see something happen to you or see you fall on your fuckin face and you don't know this about that person till you fuck around and see his hand. People/niggas hate to see you winning and when you are winning they want to be around you but not because they love you they just want to be around a winner because it will help them look good. So, stay ahead so you'll always look like you are winning. People hate undercover bad. They be mad about there situation so if they see you doing good in any kind of way, first they want to join you, then they are looking for your weakness. After they find your weakness then they feel like they can be better then you. They sit back cool it with you and wait for your fall. When you do that there happy because they feel like you're not man no more, now they can try to go on with there life. The one thing about it all is they can see you falling and they will not say shit! Stay ahead of the game.

7.15.14

Thinkin in Prison

Pain

I have no real friends—everybody I thought was my friend was only around because I had money—I'm in prison, no one really writes me like I did them when they was locked up, no one care about me like I cared about them. I haven't seen my oldest son or heard from him since our court date over the phone when I was giving up my rights and I only heard his voice in the back ground in the courtroom on that day and it was so nice to just hear his voice—I hate that my lil brother have so much time and I'm locked up myself and can't be there for him. I feel like I have no family besides my kids in my life, I feel like a lot of people want to see me down—but guess what…(I'M STILL HAPPY!) I'm a good dude, fuck them! Real shit! That shit use to bother me, but not know fuckin more. I'm "G"ed up and I'm going to stay this fuckin way til I leave this bitch, so keep on hatin on me because all it do is make me go harder—I'll never stop! Hatin' on me, I got something for that shit! The more pain I feel the harder I go! See what a lot people don't know is with pain comes a very strong mind. Love makes you weak. Pain makes you go hard..so my pain just makes me go harder and harder. Not saying I love it all the time but while I'm getting it I will make the best of it. I learn from not getting the love I want and no matter what I'm happy. I don't walk with my head down, I just stay smiling and say to myself it's going to get greater later—being disliked and feeling pain is what opened my eyes to a lot in life, it makes me not never want to do the same to people no matter what people have done to me…I'm not teaching everybody though. I might put you up on a lil game, but that's it—I don't mind sharing, I'm only going to give a way so much and keep the best for my kids or someone close to me. You always have to stay ahead of the game by five steps…you never know who out to get you! I love to hurt though, It makes me strong, I'll get love from "Jesus" because His love is the best and it last for a lifetime.

7.16.14

Dreaming in Prison

I been having good and hurtful dreams, the good ones about my second baby momma how we use to thug and vibe so good. After we vibed we would have the best sex in the world. What I loved about us viben was, it was like she was my bestfriend/lover—best sex in the world to me! The whole time me and her was able to vibe our kids wasn't really in the picture the whole time, but they did come back and we still vibe hard. The whole time I'm viben with her I know I was holding back the real love I could be giving her…not that I wasn't giving know real love, but apart of me was holding back a lil on the love I really wanted to give her. My reason for not giving the whole me was because I was scared of falling in love--- I had been thugged out and having whatever girl I wanted to. When it came down to liking one female I really didn't know what to do. I was scared and me and my baby momma did everything together. I was still scared of falling for her. I felt like it was unreal that this can really be tru that I have meet a young lady that have learnt too please me in a lot of ways. If we could keep on I know she could get better at it, so what I do I start to fuck it up because I'm scared of real love…I'm so use to always having two women just to please me, so when I got one that could, I felt like this is unreal ☺. I remember one time we was having sex and I'm getting the pussy and next thing I know it felt like it was a monster in her pussy trying to take my dick off in her and run with it. I jumped out that pussy quick as hell. I told her that shit was scary, then I told her she must have a baby in her and the baby was thinking my meat was a fuckin toy or something. He/

she wanted to play with my dick…this ain't toy baby and daddy and momma trying to have a lil fun, so I need you to roll over and go to sleep. I come to realize that, that pussy was feelin' me just that bad. That's why when a "nigga" say the pussy be bittin' that's what he mean when it feel like a monster is in that pussy. Being that she knew a lot of girls liked me I felt like she knew I liked her, so she wanted to see if she could get me to fall for her. The way I see it is a person will give to you at a time because they want to see if they can really get you to fall for them, but all at the same time in the back of their mind they be feelin' some type of way. Do he really like me, why is he liking me or spending time with me like this (when he have all these other girls crazy about him)? So, in their mind the female thinking you're trying to play with her mind and her heart. What she do is hold back her love, but all at the same time giving you the best when it comes down to the sex. She is doing that because she wants to see if she can really get you to like her or if you really like her like you are showing. "Huh yea," I like you lil momma that's why I'm giving you so much of my time, but you have to convince them (women) in their mind that you feel this type of way about them…so I started to ask myself, "Do she love me or do she think I love her (me)?" She want me to fall for her but little did she know I was! Women like to play head games just like men, but one thing about women they will leave after they feel like you have fell for them/her. It's all good though because it took eight years and to be in prison for me to want to put a ring on her finger. When you get locked up that's when a man real feelings come out. To me the good thing about it all is that I never gave her my heart all the way. I showed mad love and treated her good at times, but still held back just in case I be in a situation like this (being in prison and my feelings want to fuck with me)! I can always deal with us not being together "better" because I kept my heart and I didn't give it away even though I should have maybe, put more into "us" it all but I didn't…it is what it is though!

7.17.14

Thinking in Prison

Another day in prison---still summertime and I love it when it's hot. I like it when it's hot more than the cold because here in prison it gets real cold. Shhit it gets so cold you don't want to work out and all you want to do is stand still and try to keep warm. Now that its summertime and we can be outside I try my best to get most of my workout done outside so I can enjoy the heat. I really don't have a workout partner I mostly workout by myself and the reason being is because nobody really like to workout like I do and besides I'm determined more than a lot of these dudes. I'm not "just" working out to past time or for somebody to look at me and say, "Aye boi that dude right there stay working out." I stay working out because I have goals in life now, so I go hard unless my body shut down or if I don't feel too good. Other than that I'm at it like I'm at a boot camp—sometimes I'll get a dude that want me to workout with him, then when they see I go hard they fall off and don't want to workout with me know more. I try to stay away from them kind of peoples ---they just want to see if I can keep up ☺. Of course, I can player! I go hard buddy and don't let nothing get in my way for shit, even when I was out on the streets I was hitting the gym and sometimes I would be high as hell rollin on pills working out. It didn't matter I still got it done. The only thing about doing drugs and working out, it don't mix. I could do my workout I just wasn't putting on any mass but I was lean as hell and still cut up. Slim dude with a slim pack, but now that I'm not on no drugs I have a lil mass and it's cool to t a lil more, but I still feel like a lil dude no matter what. When I sent a picture home to my kids' baby momma wrote back saying my kids love my picture and they notice my muscles. I guess weight look better than just cut up. I workout for me, not to show out or be better than no body; I just do me. Working out help with doing my time and not only that I'm going to look good when I leave prison. When the ladies see me I want them to look at me and be like, "Damn, T Dog you still look young and fine ☺!" Then I get to pick and chose who I want, this time I'm praying and asking God to send me real woman that's going to love me, support me, like and love me for who I am because I'm always going to be T Dog no matter what. So they have no choice but, the good thing about me is I'm not going to lie to the ladies to get them or lie to get what I want from them. I'm just a Real Nigga out of the city. But yea in prison some dudes get mad, but really jealous because I go so hard with my workout. Every time they see me I'm working out and they be like damn you still at it and I tell them, "Yep, It ain't nothing else to do so I workout." Niggas be mad because they can't do what I can do and one thing about me I don't just talk about it, I be about it. If I say I'm going to do something more than likely I'm going to do it. I call it strong mind, strong body! I have a homie in here and we call him Bang and me and him stay talking about the outside world, real shit! Bang has some sisters and he feel like his sister will like a lil nigga like me. I seen a picture and I think she is sexy and hood with it just like how I like my woman to be. So me and him wrote her to see if she was down with talking to a guy like me and not only that we sent her a picture of me (before I came to prison). I told my homie when she see the picture she gone want me cause I was swagged out. Now that my hair is gone I feel like I might have to switch up the game with the clean cut swagg. Not too thugged out, more of the thug/pimp shit ☺. Still 'G' ed up tho—it make me feel good to know my dawg feel like his sister will like me out of all the dudes in here. That let me know he see a real nigga… Daily Bread---Wearing a mask that shows everything is fine, says that life's struggles are not God's design, but when we're open transparent and true, people will trust God to meet their needs too…Believers stand strong when they don't stand alone. God Bless!

7.27.14

Dreaming in Prison

My son T Dog JR, damn! Why do I have to dream about him while I'm in prison…My dream about JR was about…being that I'm down, "meaning" no money like I use to have the only car I have is my candy apple red box Chevy, no driver license. In my dream I had this bike with a motor on it and some how I ended up running into Lil T Dog somewhere with him and his mom…(This evil bitch). They were going somewhere and I was headed somewhere too and for some reason none of us was saying nothing to each other. Then all of a sudden me and T Dog said something to each other. I don't know what we said, but we could see in each other eyes that we missed each other like crazy…his mom was going to take him somewhere and I was standing right there fixing my motor bike getting ready to leave, but before I left me and T Dog was looking at each other scared and then we finally hugged then we started to cry because we haven't seen each other in awhile… Lil T Dog busted out and said to his mom that it was her fault that me and Daddy haven't been able to be around each other because you want to mean and make it hard for my real dad to see me, while I'm at your house calling your man daddy when he have his own kids (I have my own daddy). Not that I wanted to, but if I didn't call him daddy I would have been the outcast of the family so I did it--- (then I got up shaking my head like damn!) The way I feel about this whole situation is, Lord forgive me I hope the nigga die…just so he can't play daddy to my son---I'm mad as hell to have to go through this bullshit with my kids; don't know if could be worse, but I can say it's bad to me…I done prayed and prayed and still been hurting like hell about my son/kids and there is nothing going right for me. I feel like I'm building up hate in my heart because I hate to see people have to go through such pain like not being able to be with their dad and he's still alive and want to be there for his son. A nasty bitch want to come between them and let their son call another man daddy---WTF!! Lord, I need you to fix this shit for real…I want to be at peace and I damn sho' want the kids to be at peace too, ain't no tellin what these kids might go through when they grow up or feel. A lot of times they hold it in till bad "timing" or they take it out on something or someone else. These bitches don't care as long as they feel like they are hurting the next person and that's their dad. There is only one way to take this pain away—God blessed me with this fuckin $$. It might not bring my son back, but I'll show up to wherever my son be at and make sure I put some money in his pocket and money in the bank for all my kids so they'll know daddy love them. So what he (me) did was put some money in the bank for us.

7.28.14

Thinking in Prison

Another day in the chain game (prison)…one thing about me is, I grind hard as hell if it's something I want; so that means none stop up all night till I give out of gas. If I don't give out of gas I keep going and if I have the money to put my tank on full then I'm going to fill up and keep going. That's how I was when it came to my street money. When I started to sell dope I stayed up all night until I ran out of dope and I use to run out a lot. Until one day my homie told me to spend all the money I had in my pocket on dope because when you have dope you have money. I started to do that and more money I made once I put my people on my phone and I didn't have to run at cars no more. When my people would call me I was always on the way, front door service you don't even have to drive! No matter what time it was, no matter how late or early it was, sleepy and all I would get up and be there no more than 15 minutes…the good thing about me was I never really lied to my people if I was in my own car. If I'm with my home boy and me and him was riding together then it would take me a lil longer because we both was getting money. We would have to go meet his people then my people but, after I moved out from with my home boy because we stayed together at first. When I moved out and had my own car (just me) I was getting to the money all day and all night…we never really ran out of dope because we had plenty of that shit (Real Talk). That's how I was able to keep up with the dudes I was with because I stayed getting to the money. Anytime it was time to buy clothes, shoes, jewelry, rimes, cars and fuck hoes I was right in the fuckin mix (G Shit)… see my home boy was and still is that dude (Bannnggg lol) but he was /is a nigga that get money and people/haters wanted to think I was my home boy son son. Son son mean a nigga that really don't get money. Son son is a nigga that just ride in the car with a nigga that is getting money. All he do is seat on the passenger side, talk on the phone, drive wherever a nigga/home boy have to go or go make a run for his homeboy. That wasn't T Dog…I'm that nigga that's riding with my dowg and we getting this fuckin money together. We got to both look good together and not only that I will never be no fuckin do boy because I have too much swagg for that shit (Straight up!). So now that I'm on some other type of grind like working out I go hard every day. God put energy in my lil body and today a dude I know told me I can't get it all in one day. I told him 'can't' should never be in a man's vocabulary. I'll work until I run out of gas. I'm going to go hard because I'm on a fuckin mission. Like I said before I want to leave prison looking like the whole time I was away it looked like I was at a boot camp or all I did in prison was workout (I can't help it!). My nigga Boosie said, "Get ya weight up so when them cameras flash you don't have to worry about shit, your ready for whatever." Have you ever seen a lil nigga that walk with confidence? That's me T Dog nigga! I got to get this fuckin $$ so I have to go hard and be consistent! I get it all until I run out. Fuck stopping or sleeping I gotta get it! When I look back at my life when I was getting money in the streets, now when I think about it I did have a point to prove and that was to show every motherfucker that might have looked down on me or felt like I was going to be in prison because of my bad attitude. I wanted to show them I'll take the risk of going out there in the streets to get money and live how I felt like I should live. No matter if later on I ended up blowing the money but, I can look back and say I lived a lil bit of my fuckin life. Thanks to God because He is the one that made it all possible. What God did was let me enjoy the street money and after He felt like it was time to stop He put a stop to it and made it to where He wanted me to make money the right way. That way I can last long out here in the world and be there for my kids… Dope money make a nigga want mo money!

8.6.14

Thinking in Prison

I love reading my Bible because the more I read it; it feeds my mind, body and soul. After the officer comes in and do head count and they clear count I get up and drink some coffee and be ready to read my bible. As I'm reading it, it always be things in the Bible that relates to my life, my past or someone I talk to lie and as I read it something comes over me that says write or write to or talk to that person that might be having a lil problem in their life. So what I do is I say to myself, "Lord, I'll do it when the opportunity comes." I don't be in no rush too do it, I just wait on the Lord to make a way for me to do it then I make my move---like my home boy here; me and him may chop it up and he'll put me up on game and I'll put him up on game but, one thing I notice about me talking to him is I never feel like it really be T Dog speaking. I be feeling like it be Jesus speaking through me and I tell him that too. He tell me that I speak very well and I keep it real and positive. I asked my home boy, "How do he feel about my response and the feed back I give him," and that's when he tell me, "That I do good when giving a person feedback," all I do is smile and tell him "thank you." I want to go to school when I get out of prison for Current Social Problems or Marriage & Family because I love to talk and help people with their problems or be someone they can talk too because I don't mind listening…I'm good with listening that's why a lot of people love to talk to me. When I was young my big cousin would always ride and talk to me and all I would do is listen to everything he would talk about and all I would be following alone. Just in case he was to ask me something about something he just said, I could tell him so he would know I'm listening. I feel like my brother Boosie when he said (God put me here to feed people, I know he did.) That's how I feel. God put me here to feed people just like brah (Boosie). Just in a different way. Boosie touch us through his songs and I'm going to touch people when I talk to them. One thing I have noticed in life is that a lot of people really don't want to find out about Jesus like that, they have their own beliefs about their life. When I hear their problem I say to myself, "Damn, they need to find Jesus." Like the song say, "Jesus is real I know the Lord been good to me." I know what God will and can do in our life and your life if you believe in Him and His son. Not only that turn your life around or turn your heart from bitter to good. Know matter what may happen in your life rather good or bad still give God praise because He know what He is doing. Let Him have His way, don't be mad and turn on Him, still thank Him and I know it might seem hard to do but, it can be done…I feel like a lot of times God curse us for whatever His reason might be and then He have the ones that are chosen in His eyes so He keep them safe. I do feel like it's a big test and we are just passing through.

8.7.14

Just got done eating a soup and tuna altogether before I go to bed. After eating and drinking some water I said, "Thank you Lord and thank you Lord for my cousin because he have been looking out for me every since I contacted him." It feels so good to go to bed full and then you think about the person that put money on your books, so you can eat as good as you are eating. I am very thankful of him damn! That's my nigga! One thing about being in prison or should I say this fuck ass camp and these fuck niggas be thinking they're going to be the only ones get love in this bitch, like can't nobody else get love in here….lol, they got me fucked up! I might not be getting visits but I do have food in my locker to eat. One thing about me is I know how to save until I want to eat good and when I want to eat real good that's when I do the soup and tuna with some crackers. These bitch ass niggas be mad lol. I can see it on their face and you know what I do I just smile to myself and say, "Thank you, Lord for putting it in my cousin heart to even do what he do for me." The first time I even wrote cuz I really never really said to put money on my books. I just told him that if he want to that he could if he had it and in three or four days cuz had done put a $100 on my card…lol. I was happy has hell!!! A $100! I could buy anything I wanted and I did. I was so happy and felt fucking loved by my cousin, my big cousin that I use to ride with when I was a teenager…this nigga still in my life and have been since have meet him. We might not agree on everything but as far as him keeping it real at a time I need him he is there. My only thing is how can I ever show him love back is what I keep asking myself. The only thing I can say is, I have to get rich so I can take my cousin somewhere and we have mad fun or buy him a nice ass car he has always wanted. I know that it will make him happy as shit. The thing is I'm not paying him back because when real niggas do something for you they do it from the heart, so you never had to pay them back. If you ever get the chance you show that person mad love back…cuz done ordered me Ebony magazines and I'm trying to get him to hook me up with one of his ladies friends that's up there in the city with him. If he do that I'm really in there because in my mind I'm only going back to see my kids and after that hopefully I be on my way to the city where it's all going down at. It feels good having a cuz here having a nigga back but, all at the same time cuz going through it his self. I can tell by what he be saying in the letters he write me. He don't say, "Aye, Cuz I know you know how to get money so when you get out don't even play. Get out, catch up with your kids, get a job and be on your way to the TOP… Once I hook you up with on of my lil lady friends up here in the city, you'll be straight. I know you one real nigga and you won't let me down when I hook you up with her." I know she's going to be thinking Billy is going to try to hook me up with a jail bird and he don't even know I ain't even with it. I'm going to see who his cousin is and that's when cuz is suppose to have her google me so she'll see who I be. Then have her to write me…cuz be like, "Yea cuz try to learn this and that and when you get out you know it's going to be hard so get ready for it." In my head and when I wrote him back I was like, Cuz, I don't think it's going to be hard. I feel like I'm going to get right back to the money. I'll have a more of a clear mind then before and while I have the clear mind I'll attack my plans that I have. I'll stay on the right path because I already know one slip and I'm outta here, back in jail or prison. I know I have to stay on the right path and think clear… If I feel like or even put in my head that it's going to be hard, I feel like that's when the crazy thinking is going to start coming. What I do is I'm going to do my thing when I walk out them gates. I'm not telling cuz to lie to me but, be more uplifting then what he is doing…real shit! I really don't want to hear the bullshit about it's going to be hard (fuck that!). Close mouths don't get feed and I know how too run mine G shit… I did write him back and told him that I feel like everything is going to be all good with me. It will be even better if he hooked me up with one of them shawtys.

8.11.14

Thinking in Prison

I never seen so many under cover fagots in my life but, prison do have them and these pussy ass niggas have girlfriends. WTF!! What gets me is they will seat and talk to you about women all day, then they will get up and you'll see the bitch in them. Like how he walk, you'll see them rub on himself or stay looking in the mirror. I be saying to myself like what the fuck are you looking for…these fuck ass niggas love to be seen and all but, the bad part is they like to be seen by dudes. Then when they have a visit they act like their so into with their woman. These fuck ass niggas be killing me and if you take a liking to one of them because you think he might be cool. The nigga see you choppin it up with the next dude then the bitch ass nigga want to get in his feelings about that shit. Then you know this bitch ass nigga got bitch in him. I can deal with the guys that you know are guy because you know but, the ones that want to come talk to you just to see what type of time you're on is what gets me…that's one thing I hate about this prison I'm at because I was hoping I was going to meet a/or some real ass niggas. All I'm seeing is some undercover gay ass niggas that get in their feelings like a hoe ass nigga…I was hoping I would meet a nigga I can play cards with so time would fly by fast but, nooo every nigga I have came across is weak and have gay ass ways. I don't even have a workout partner because for one: either there are a haters, like I say don't go hard like me. So they stay away from me as much as they can and when they build up enough nerve then they might want to come fuck with me "a G" or do a lil workout. It would be cool to have somebody to workout with so we can push each other and motivate each other but, nooo they just want to get around me and just talk about their lil life. I think to be up in a man's face and be hoping the dude change for the better of him…fuck no gay ass nigga. Where I'm from we ain't weak we love the ladies and we don't get down like that homie. Keep on acting and talking the way you are all out the side of your neck, I'll expose your gay ass.

8.12.14

Thinking in Prison

One thing I have found out about this prison/work camp I'm at is dudes will play up under you rather it's for the good or bad. The good is for them and the bad is for you but the bad is not really bad if you can see the bullshit before it comes your way. The good for them is they ease themselves up under you by trying to befriend you and the reason for them doing that is because they are lacking somewhere in this fucking prison with something. Rather if it's they can't get on the phone and they see that you can or you smoke without asking anybody because you have your own money. You can go buy canteen anytime you get ready; you get visits a lot and they see that. That is some of the reasons why they will try to befriend you because they feel like you got it and you don't need nobody for shit. Now they want to be your friend or just try to talk to you about anything or somebody else and want you to feel them on what they are saying. One thing about T Dog is I watch "everything." If you are coming to talk to me about something or somebody nine times out of ten you'll also talking about your damn self. One thing about being in here you have to stay on guard at all times but, don't look like it. The reason for faking is so a nigga will think you are dumb or lame ass fuck. Not only that you acting that way because all at the same time he is thinking can he get over on you; You looking at him for one: figuring him out and you trying a way to be able to use his dumb ass. It's called thinking better than his dumb ass. The good part about it all is, you can see all the bullshit that's been brought to you. So you know how to play the pussy nigga, because real know real and real know bullshit. So when these niggas come my way I can see right through they fake ass and play right against them. Even the weak ass undercover ass gay niggas, for me when they come my way and want to always talk about girls knowing damn well they ass is gay. Once I peep game I'll talk a lil bit and find out about them and their family to see if they have somebody they can hook me up with like their sister or mom shhit I don't give a fuck. After I do that and it work or not I get away from they gay ass. See while you think you're out smarting me I'm outsmarting you bitch nigga…In prison you have to be on your shit, if you ask me because you have too watch out for the snakes and the snakes be the main people smiling in your face. I stay to myself and wait for these bitch ass niggas to come to me with the bullshit and you best believe they will come. When they do I listen and when it don't sound right or it look funny or sound funny that's when I start to plot on them…all they be trying to do is use anybody they can in anyway so you have to be careful. Just as I was writing this a dude from my city came up to me and asked me to come eat with him and I'm like "wow" because you don't get that everyday. We from the same city but we don't even know each other, he just came up to me and offered me to eat with him and I said, "okay" and we ate. This one dude that ain't from my city came to me talking about somebody owe him and how dude haven't paid him back, then later that night he was borrowing from me and it only was a mayo. He tell me he gone pay me back today and this nigga haven't did it yet. I was going to tell the nigga that he didn't have to pay me back because it was just a mayo. He said he was going to, so I'm just seating back waiting…it's funny to me because he's one of these cats in here that thinks he has it going on, but stay borrowing from the next man. The next time he wants to borrow I'll tell him I can't because he's not a man of his word. You have to be a man of your word no matter what you borrow from anybody because if you don't pay that person back when you say you will, you done fucked up. Thank God I haven't had to borrow from one of these dudes I don't know and if I don't have I just don't have it because I'm not borrowing anyways.

8.15.14

Thinking in Prison—Is There Hope?

In real life do I think, I'm the good guy…No! I'm the bad guy I just have some bad ways about myself. Being in this fucking prison for me I can only think so far and all you really can do is think about what you what to do when you get out of here or think about your past. Like things you have done in the past....shhit I'm tired of thinking it's like I'm running my mind crazy, I think about a lot of things I should of did in my past. Then I start "thinking" like when I was in my past and some way I was doing great, but when I look bad I be saying "Damn" I wish this or I should have done this or that this way, but that's in the past and now I have to live for my future. As I'm in prison thinking about my future I get a lil scared to leave prison because I'm what it's going to be like for me. Not saying it's going to be all bad just don't want to have to come back to prison all by it's self. One thing I noticed back in my past is when I started to go to jail it's like I never stopped going. Now that I have made it to prison I see a lot these dudes that have been back more than once, two, and three times. I don't want to be one of them dudes that keep on coming back like that. One thing I do know is how I did keep going to jail back in my past is because I was young and I called myself thuggin' and didn't really give a fuck. When I got out of jail I would go back and do the same thing that put me in jail. Now I know better shhit, I knew better than I just didn't think about it as much as I think about it now or maybe I feel like I have a big reason to stay out. Maybe because I think I can be in the three kids that I have left in my life. Maybe I see the big picture now and now I want to be all I can be. I don't need no fuck up's because I do want to see if I can get the real money and the real money is not that street money because Ima tell you the truth we cannot outsmart the cops, there hiding dudes that keep getting out doing the same thing. I want that money that's going to keep you free, that working money even though it might take a lil longer. It's still worth it if you have kids or a family. I guess all I'm asking is, "Is there hope for my life?" For me to stay out of jail or prison, to be around all my kids, to make my life out of something and to make my brothers happy. I'm asking, "Is there really hope?" Lord, I need you to please help me to keep my faith and keep on doing what's right but, also keep me away from all the people that want to see me lose. If not I'm going to come out my being nice stage and give them what they are asking for...I'm going stay strong and try my very best to keep my head up and keep on smiling. Without you Lord, I don't know what

I'll do…the shorter I get to going home the harder it gets for me. I'm getting for very tired of being around all these fuck as dudes. FUCK!

8.16.14

One thing I notice about people is that they change like the fuckin weather. Like theses dudes I'm in prison wit, really these fuck ass niggas I'm in prison with are some wanna be cool, wanna be thug, wanna be cool nigga but, all at the same time this nigga is gay bitch nigga. I don't know what it is about lil old me but, these bitch ass niggas either hatin or in their feelings for what ever reason…even the niggas from your own city hate on you but, I know why the niggas from your city hate. They hate because they know what you was doing out there in the streets and they wish it was them and since it wasn't them they mad at you or they just have hatin in their bitch ass. The niggas that you don't know they hate for almost the same reason but, being that I'm in prison and I'm around all these different pussy niggas I can see how they change it up. One minute they want to be cool with you until yall have to keep being around each other, being now you live with this pussy nigga. Y'all have to do time together and you can see how this pussy nigga is in real life…I'll give you an "example," like a nigga will come vibe with you or workout with you just to see how strong you are because he done seen you on the pound doing your thing. He just haven't been able to get close to you to talk to you to see way your mind is at. When he do get a chance to talk to you the first thing he say to be cool with you for the moment is, "Yea, I be seeing you going hard," and I be saying, "Damn, do you go hard." The next thing you know these folks move you right next to this cat and now you living with him, so you can really see how this pussy nigga is and you don't see the pussy in this nigga until you be there for a lil bit then the nigga start to unfold. What he do is offer for yall to workout together just to see if he can out do you and when it ball down to it he can't. Then you start to see the nigga be some timing. At first you thought the nigga was cool, but really deep down the nigga hate that you go harder than him. So guess what he do, he back away and don't want to workout with you. Now all both of y'all are back to working out by y'all self because one thing about niggas is they want and they love to feel like they are better than you. If they feel like they are not better than you the first thing they do is be mad and hate on you but, the reason why I call them pussy nigga is because they hate undercover just like they are gay undercover...they are bitches in real life. These fuck niggas really have bitch ways, like when I was saying they only want to talk to you to see where you're at. Like, what you wanna do when you get out of here and if you seem like you are the type of person that go hard and they see that. That mean nine times out of ten any and everything that comes out your mouth is so real. They know deep down in their heart they ain't like you or go harder than you, they are mad at you first then themselves! They mad at themselves because they don't want to hate but, they can't help it because they feel like nobody should be or go harder than them and that eat at them. They have this hate in their heart that they can't get rid of until they feel like they might be better than you or someone else they hating on. What they do is workout by themselves to try to get ahead of the game and when they feel like they are ahead that's when they come back to talk to you so they can see if y'all can be cool and maybe try this friendship shit again. See hatin on me boiii you in trouble like a motha fucka because one thing about me is I go harder than a bitch and if I ever see a weak ass nigga want to try to be better than me "T Dog" I take that shit to cloud 9 and I tell that nigga to catch up...this shit real over here homeboy and one thing about me is I don't compete unless I'm going to win some money or something. Other than that I stay in my own lane and do me. One thing about me is I don't just do this shit in prison I do this shit on the outs too so it's really nothing to me...I do this.

8.21.14

Thinking in Prison

Sometimes when I go to the bathroom to pee sometimes I look down but, not really at my dick I just look down to make sure I'm shooting this pee in the right spot. Today was a lil different after a workout a lot of times you feel a lot better for yourself and that's because you have put your body to work for something good and all at the same time as you go on and on with your workout your body start to change for the good. Whatever it is you are working start to grow bigger and you start to get stronger. One thing about working out is once you put it in your head this is what your going to be doing and that is stay working out to change your body into better shape then that's what's going to happen. See people think just because you workout it only gives you big muscles, but that's not all working out do to your body. Working out also builds your confidence, it makes you feel a lot healthier, it may even help with your skin the way it look... you just never know how your workout will help your body and how you will feel about yourself until you put it in your head that you're going to workout and get in better shape. Once you do it and not stop you will start to see what I am talking about. As for me I went to the bathroom today and pee'ed and when I grabbed my dick it felt healthy as hell and I'm shaking my dick off, but as I'm shaking I'm saying to myself, "Damn, my dick feel healthy and plus it's a nice size." Then I start to think like, "Damn, my dick have been locked up for a long fuckin time (Damn)!" The thing about my dick is I have a nice piece of meat and I can't do shit wit this bitch right now because I'm locked up. Then I start to think to myself how some of the ladies have told me that I have a pretty dick. All I can do is shake it and put him away til I'm released and until I find the right woman that's going to love it and be crazy about it. So I can give her the best sex of her life and if I like her more and more I have more to give her. Being in prison will make you think of some freaky shit. I really want to eat me some pussy but, she has to have that water type pussy and she might even have to be my lady because that on-to-go sex I really ain't feeling no more now that I'm older. I feel like if I'm going to give myself away like that why not be wit her so she can have T Dog all to herself...I guess all I'm saying is that I need some pussy BAD!

8.22.14

Thinking in Prison

When you're all alone and there is no one but you. You have to teach yourself or notice what God has put in your mind or heart to do. Sometimes it's hard to know if God is speaking to you because you don't really hear nobody. So you start to think to yourself and then you realize that it's God if it's good or positive that you're thinking about because God is only going to put good and positive in your mind and heart. What I'm really talking about is how I'm going to be when I get out of prison. One thing for sure I know I still have a lot more happiness in me and the thing about it, it just come out the blue and then I have them days where I'm just sitting back quite and being in my zone, not really thinking but, thinking---if you know what I mean. I guess it will be days like this rather you in or out of prison. All I know is I want and I'm going to make sure I have better days and live with a lot more peace than I have ever did. I can say the Lord has blessed me with some very good days of my life. So I'm not going to complain about me being locked up or being away from my kids. I'm going to say, "Thank you Lord," because all you (God) you are doing is teaching your child about life so I can teach others. I do think about rather I want a lady meaning a girlfriend or do I want to just do me and be into my career. All I know is two heads are better than one and if I get a girlfriend we can help each other grow, love each other, motivate each other, and make sure the both of us are and stay happy. Now I can still be in will be happy rather I have a girlfriend or not. All I'm saying is if the right one comes alone (woman) I'm going to vibe. I'm not going to look for her, I'm going to let God send this one because when I look back I feel like I haven't been doing a good job---So I'm going to chill and work on me and my career and what I need out of life for my kids and me. In order for her (woman) to be my girlfriend she damn sho' gone have to be on point with understanding me and giving me the right love or maybe a love I never even had before—I can deal with that! Now, I don't want no just anybody because she is sweet, she has to be more than just sweet. She has to have some clean wet water type pussy and be pretty. She has to love herself and God then I can love her. These are some of the things I look for in a beautiful woman. I have a street nigga swag, a dope boy hustle and a heart like God want me to have. Do I want anymore kids? Only if she have one or maybe if she can make me believe she want take our child away from me when she get mad, then yes I would love more—I can say I am scared. Scared of what might happen if we don't be together and how it will effect our child...now that I have had my freedom taken away from me for these 18 months I can say when I live prison I'm going to make sure I make everyday count. I'm going to make sure I think before I make a move like the game chess. When I was younger I use to move fast without thinking too much or maybe not at all. I would just go and learn later, but now I'm older and have to think ahead and slow everything down just a lil so I won't be doing all this falling and getting up type shit! I want to walk into peace and wave to all my worries good-bye.

8.31.14

Thinking in Prison

The mind of T Dog—growing up I never really dreamed big. All I did was lived to see how far I was going to go in life and I can say as of now I have came pretty far. Being that I have been through foster homes and in and out of jail, even prison. I've been in the streets selling of kinds of drugs, running into police because I didn't have DL's, niggas wanting to rob me because I was getting money in the streets and with all the money I was making when I look back, I never had any real or big goals in life. I was just living life not knowing how far I was going to go...as time went on, I ran into the street money because of the friend I had. That's pretty much how he made money is from the streets. Being around him it was easy for me to get street money because at the time the street money was so easy to get. For me I started and it didn't take me long before I caught on to the street life and selling drugs. Now in the midst of me selling drugs I took loses and would go to jail for driving without license but, I would bond out and go back to doing the same thing and that's driving. Until I said to myself, "Fuck it, I'm going to stop driving so much" and I did that. I couldn't get my DL's at the time because child support was stopping that. One time I did catch up on my child support and got my DL's back but, after some time had went by I still ended up losing them again. My thing was with the last foster home I was at and that's my Grandma house, I never thought about college, shhit no one there never asked me, "Did I ever want to go?" and my cousin which is my grandma nephew never put me up on these types of things. So, to me that left me alone to make a way on my own. When I meet my so called friend at the time being around him we hung, got money and fucked all the girls we liked. With me following him or being around him it's like we was alike and did the same thing and everything alike. Something was telling me as time went on me and him was not alike for some reason because in my mind it's like I wanted to find out more to what was going on in life. Some type of way I stayed around him/the people I knew. A lot of people knew him and when we became friends we stayed together, so when you seen him you seen me. It was all good but, some people hated on us because we was so tight. The only thing I could learn from him was the streets and he still kept some of that from me. My cousin he would put me up on shit but, it wasn't nothing that would help me in the long run. Tell me cuz go take up some college courses or try this or try that and if he say he did I damn sho' don't remember him telling me these things. Once I started to sell dope and making my own money it's like my cousin ended up doing the shit with me and he was ten years older. One time I went to jail and left him my phone so he could keep my money going. He did it but, he didn't do it like a street nigga would work my phone. He made it like it was a business and the reason why he ran it like this is because he not a street nigga. I mean he have been around street dudes but, he is not a street nigga. That's why he ended up moving to another state and have a 'job' because he already knew to get a lil money and get out the game before he ended up in prison. As I'm getting older I'm starting to notice a lot now about life and what to do when you're getting fast money; you save and think far ahead, have goals in life so when you want to better your life you know more than just the streets. It's like how they tell the NFL players to go to college and take something just in case football don't workout for them so they can have something to fall back on. Same thing with the street life, have a back-up plan so you won't have to sell dope all your life or until you get all them years in prison. Think of a plan, get fast money and make your plan work and get out of the game. Peace!

8.31.14

Pt.2

My cousin said in this lil book he wrote, "He always wanted someone on the same mind frame as him." When it came to life and getting money. God blessed him with that and that person was me. One thing about me, I could peep game to the point where he didn't have to say nothing. Now that I'm older and can see more clear, he stayed ahead of me not just because he was older but, because he knew things I didn't know. In his mind he wasn't going to put me up on the things he knew. There is no telling how far I would go with the things he could have taught me. What he did was kept the good to himself and kept me in the blind with coming to pick me up and riding with me all around. Taking me here or there, showing me he wasn't scared to holla at the girls. I guess he felt like if he do these things I would think he is so real. One thing about a younsta is they do grow up sooner than you think and when they do they start to see things a lot more clearer. To me it's best to keep it all the way real with a kid so when they grow up they can look back and say, "Damn, brah kept it so real with me." Then they won't see no flaws in you. When looking back til now I feel like my cousin played me and then I feel like this nigga must think I'm a damn fool! I might make you think I'm a fool but, I have more sense than a lil bit. Now being that I'm in prison yes, he sent me money but, what gets me is the thing I asked him for I haven't gotten yet. Then he wants to write me to tell me what I need to be learning while in prison and have a lot of time on my hands so I need to learn as much as I can.

All of these things he is telling me now I already know and been doing. He been telling me, "Think of this as a good thing" and as I'm reading it I have this look on my face like, "Man, come on, I already know this shit. Tell me some shit I don't know." Why didn't you tell ne this when I had money or a long time ago? I guess you didn't want to do that because of what? I probably would have did all the good you would have put me on. I don't know, all I know is real love from that bullshit. Just to keep a nigga cool with you because deep down you know you could have gave a nigga more game. So giving it to me now it really don't mean shit. What I need now is some money and for you to hook me up with one of these females from the city! Fuck all that teaching shit you talking about Cuz, I been on all that you been talking about and no I don't look at being here as a bad thing. I'm going to learn from this and move forward in life. One thing that he did put me up on was the acting and with my own mind I went into modeling first. Being that he put me up on it I went and did it and everything I started to do as far as the modeling came out good. All I have to do is keep going and do better…to keep it real I was made for the cameras. I have that smile that will make anybody smile even if you're mad ☺ and I might be a lil cute. That's what the girls have told me, I am a keeper. I have the body and now all I need is the right deal and I can live now. Peace!

9.7.14

Thinking in Prison

I've been thinking about my past life and now that I'm older, I can really understand what was going on in my teenage days. My grandma kids the (boys) never asked me or cared to ask me and my brother what we wanted to be when we grow up, not that I can remember I can say I really didn't know what I wanted to be). At the time I do remember one of her sons having us in the back yard talking shit to us about not giving his mom a hard time and that we need to be doing something with ourselves. Being that my brother was older than me dude was trying to talk my brother into going into the fucking army (like him).

My brother wasn't wit that shit at all and for me he never asked me what was I into at the time to see if I was good at this or that. All he was doing in my eyes was telling us that we need to do or think of something, but while we was back there (yard) dude was digging a hole—I think we was cleaning a lil bit back there and for some reason I wasn't feeling the conversation at all. It had me with a lil attitude because it was like he was threatening us in some kind type and I didn't like that shit at all! It's like grandma told him to get us back there to talk with us and get us back there to scare us. Not that we was, but he was not no dude we thought was cool to vibe with. Now that I'm older and understand more better, yea he was asking us these questions back then but what he was really doing was trying to get us out of his moms house. Also letting us know yall want be here for long so we better think of something. As I can recall we never picked to come to ya'll momma house, DCF put us there and not only that ya'll mom took a liking to us and adopted us. That means we are hers to! Grandma kids seen that she took a liking to us so what they did at first was try to scare us, no help and talk down on grandma/their mom about us so grandma can feel some type of way, so it would be easy for her to kick us out when we got older enough. For my brother he never was there anyways he stayed in the streets, for me I stayed getting in just a lil bit of trouble in school or on the bus. I guess that made grandma mad or look bad because she had to come get me from school sometimes—I was still young doing these things, but as I got older and was about 18 years old it was like we had to go get out. Grandma would put it on me for being bad or kept getting in trouble. That's not the case if you ask me; I mean we are your kids too! And you made it this way so luckily I had a friend I could go live with but, we no longer stayed wit grandma. To me it was like they all was waiting for us to turn 18 so we could leave because once you turn 18 they can either kick you out or you're welcome to leave. Without having help like that from her kids it was hard for us/me to really get a good job and I did get a job at this store for a little while and I would walk or rode my bike to get there. I used that money to buy me shoes, now I'm not saying that my grandma was not there for us because she was and she did good. I do believe that her kids got into her head because they was a lil jealous that their mom toke a liking to us (me and my brothers) and wanted all the attention, but I say that to say this, "I feel like I was force just a lil bit to the streets because the only friend I had and acted like he cared, came and got me and let me live with him, his mom and that was in the hood." After being in the hood cause what is going to happens if you live in the hood? You will start to do hood shit, if you live around folks that have good jobs guess what you'll end up with a good job and being that I stayed in the hood I started the hood shit and never stopped until I got older and seen where you could end up at (if you don't make a change in your life). Now that I I'm not in the hood I was in prison all I could do is think about my whole life and the path I took. I'm not saying that I regret any of my life because I really love my life and the things I experienced, but all it showed me was think ahead. Plan for the future don't just ball for the moment; think about what you can have ten years of now. Do I blame anybody for me doing the things I choose to do? No! I did them because I chose to, but also because of who I was around too. So, from me to you to anybody that's reading this surround yourself around the crowd/people that's doing what your doing but I'm going to tell you this, "If it's bad then bad is what your going to get back out of it, if it's good then you'll receive good." And it will long and you won't have to worry about being in prison or jail unless you do something crazy. Other than that you gone be good! One thing I have noticed is a lot of people won't teach you, show you or tell you shit if you already don't know. They will keep it from you until you find out yourself. That's why I say mother's and father's make sure you tell your kids what they are good at, how pretty they is, how nice of a smile they have. Teach them how to cook and then tell them if the food was good and what they left out so they can make it better. All of these things will help your kids in the long run with life. Ask them what do they want to be when they get older and still give your input on what you think so they can later think about it also. I was a young kid before and these are some of the things I felt like I was missing out on in my younger days. I never knew I was cute, I never knew I had a nice smile and the list go on and on. How I look at it now is, I'm older and now I know what's good about me and how things look and I feel a whole better now that I know and being that I have been through now I can pass it on to my kids, so they'll know how pretty and handsome they are or how good they are at football, basketball or whatever sport they be in. I'm just going to be there to tell them how good they are and help them to become better. I been through a lot, but I have also seen better days it's just when they came I lived for the moment and not for the long ride. My reason for telling the parents all these things is because now that I'm older I sometimes be thinking it might be too late for me to have a dream and also make it come true. Now sometimes it seems like it's going to take to long to reach my goals and I'm running out of time. Also, my look is just a lil older then when I was young and fresh, but I still have faith and I'm still alive so I'm going to keep on going... even though I'm getting old I still feel like I have what it take to be in a movie, to be on a cover of a magazine or anything I put my mind I'm even in better shape than I was when I was young...so to me I still got it and not only that the way people look at me tells me a lot ☺ all smiles.

Thinking in Prison

My real name is T Dog! When we was took (me and my brothers) from our mom, they lady me and my brothers ended up staying with; we change our last name to her last name. I guess only to feel like we was really apart of the family at the time, but when I got older and really understood life and understanding my real mom background I started to say to myself, "I'm really not my adopted family." Not saying they are bad people or anything, but I'm not like them! I'm like my mom and she is a *TRU*! My family have had it hard every since they been coming up. As I got around them I seen how really nobody in the family had anything. Now that I'm older I see all my family has is that we all have very bad attitudes (out of this world). Not saying that's a good thing, but I can say that, "That's us." I love it because that's my family. I love my family deep in my heart and being that me and my brothers really didn't really grow up around a lot of my family; it made some of my family feel like we was too good or we didn't want to be keen for whatever reason. That's not the case we just all grew up different, so when I came back around to my family some of them looking all mad like I owe them something. I'm not the reason why me and my brothers didn't grow up around y'all so don't be mad at me. I still love all of y'all no matter how long I been gone. For some reason only some of us get alone...now I can say that even though I am family I'm not like some of them in a lot of ways. I have the attitude, but I been trying to better myself in life ever since I can remember. I see where I could be if I didn't try to change my ways and how I act. I'm glad God saved me and my brothers and put us in a foster home because being that my mom was using drugs ain't no telling where we would be today. Even though (me and all my brothers) all of us ended up in prison I feel like it could be a whole lot worse...now that I'm thinking real hard about changing my name from my adopted name back to my biological name, I'm also thinking about doing a clothing line with using my name. Now I don't know how hard it's going to be to do this, but it's something I want to try. I feel like my name is a very catchy name and also if I come out with a clothing line with it and it's hot I think I can do numbers. There is some things I'm going to have to find in order to build my brand like, what kind of clothes I want to bring out. I really think I know what I want I just have to find or build a team to see what kind of ideas we can come up with.

9.15.14

Thinking in Prison Pt.1

Been thinking---Why can't I find a real nigga that's on the same shit I'm on? I'm in prison and I see a lot and a lot of what I see is these niggas be hatin like shit. How I know is, for one I can see it in their eyes and how they talk to me. With me being me I be knowing they have this hatin shit in their blood, but all at the same time I keep it cool as long as they ain't disrespecting me. What they do is be undercover hatin but, be in your face like everything is so cool. When really they either want to be you, be like you or be better than you or even hate that they feel like they know or feel like you the shit! One thing about me is, I know and also feel like I am a threat to some of these niggas because I'm a cool ass nigga and they might be cool too, but one thing about me is I want hate on the next man. If anything I will tell him, "You swagged up homie." Shhit, why not? Being in prison and being in around all these dudes I watch their every move, how they act, how they walk and what they like to talk about. When they hold a conversation with me how they move their hands to express their self and the list goes on and on. I do that to see what is this nigga intention is when he is speaking to me—a lot or some people/niggas like to come talk to me to see if I'm a down ass nigga. Then you have the ones that will come talk to me to see where my head is. Then you have the ones that will come to me so they can talk about positive things. Then you have the ones that want to see if they can come trick me and try to make me thing they are real but, like I had always had said, "One thing about a real nigga is he can feel or see the bullshit before he fall for anything." So to me he really wasting his time coming to me with the bullshit because I see it and the thing about it all once I see you on the bullshit I'll play right up under your ass like you the damn fool! The thing that gets me is niggas from around your way (way you from) they gone be against you but, all at the same time make like ya'll cool just a lil bit because we from the same city. That's how they get down in prison and all at the same time you know this nigga ain't really right because in real life outside of prison on the streets this nigga act like he was better than you. Now that ya'll are in prison he don't mind being in cool with you---so ya'll start to talk and chill but, all at the same time you keeping your eye on this nigga cause you know what he was on before you got to prison but, ya'll keep chopping it up and he let you in a lil bit and you let him in a lil bit. One thing about a nigga that thinks he better is they talk more so I seat back and listen. Also give a lil bit so he can give me more---now things you/I be giving me real but, you start to notice everything you say you're going to do he say he was going to do it or he'll try to say something better---then you say to yourself like damn this nigga want to do everything I want to do but, really want to do it better. One thing I have known is you is you can only be you and I only can be me. So know matter how better you try to be over me I'm still different in my own way, so you're no threat to me it just let me know that I'm on the right path and I'm going to keep on going. One thing about a fake nigga is he will show you his hand and you best believe I am looking to see what you have in your hand because I need to know "nigga" and that's when one day you will see the nigga acting funny with you. It don't be one of them days where a nigga might be stressing because I know the difference. It's one of them days you see the real side of that nigga and he can't hide it. I'll let ya'll in on something, one thing about a fake ass nigga and you know he ain't real a lot of times you can tell by this nigga hand shake. If you ain't feeling his hand shake nine times out of ten it ain't no love, he's up to something. Always be on the lookout. See you have to be able to read bullshit at all times because you don't need no bitch ass nigga trying to play up under you and he could be trying for all kinds of reasons. For me I think a nigga be trying to keep me from his bitch! Lol Like I have said before, "Never think you are playing up under a real nigga because really he is playing under you in all ways!" Sometimes I ask myself, "Why don't I have friends like that?" Then I answer myself and say, "Ain't nobody real like me, if they are real I haven't meet them yet." The only ones I know is real is some rappers, like my brother from another mother Boosie, Yo Gotti and Young Jeezy that's just a few to name real quick ya feel me? I feel like I'm all alone---till I get this fuckin money then everybody gone be acting real lol.

Thinking in Prison

Pt. 2

One thing my lil dawg told me in here is the reason why niggas/people hate on you is because you roc'ed up, I still look young and I stay to myself---cause I told him I don't know why people hate on me and that's when he told me why they hate. I told him I stay to myself because it's something about my look or something that make these niggas/people hate on---sometimes I think to myself like, "I can't be all that for niggas to just stay away from me like that." I guess so, because after a lil conversation with me them niggas/people be gone in the wind. I guess to some I might look like you can fed that bullshit to so they be wantin to see and when I open my mouth and speak they be looking and feeling crazy. Like damn, dude is head strong! This one dude be telling me I need to read this book and it will tell me all about religion and this and that. I told dude, "Nah, I'm good." The only book I'm going to read is my Bible, that's it. I believe in what I believe and you believe what you believe. I'm not wit reading about this and that so my head can be all fucked up, I'm going to stay on my same path because in the Bible it do say people will try to trick you and lead you down the wrong path. I'm not fixing to be reading no book so it can get me off my Jesus our God because He has been so goo to me and I know it. These niggas in here are double minded and don't give a fuck about a nigga. All they wanna see is you fuck anyway possible. That's why they stay away from me and I stay away them because I know they are evil and what I'll do is test them like, I'll ask them to teach me how to play chest just to see if they'll do it and a nigga want teach me shit! All he want to do is beat me cause he love to win and feel like he's ahead. For me I don't mind to lose (some) but, you best believe when I get the hang of it I will end up winning or getting better. One thing about it all to me is winning means being unafraid to lose. Do I talk to myself? Yes! Am I crazy? Hell no!

9.21.14

Thinking in Prison

Something I noticed about in prison is when your on your way out it can get a lil tougher. Being that everybody already know you don't have long left it seems like a lot of people want to give you a hard time and the officers can be the main ones. Boii, they will talk to you any kind of way make you clean up shit that has nothing to do with what you're suppose to be doing and if you say something then they will tell your ass to shut up or shut the fuck up. You'll be looking like who the fuck you talking to but, you have to change that look on your face and either smile or look straight face and say, "Yes sir or no sir." Deep down inside you be wanting to beat their ass but, you can't. If you keep talking trying to explain your self they'll tell you if you don't shut up or I'll lock your ass up. Now, you know you don't want to go to lock up because it's hot or either too cold over there and when I say hot I mean hot! Not only that depending on what they say you did you might not eat or eat to good. For me it's been going just a lil hard but, not hard enough for me to go off on one of the officers and for them to send me to lock up and don't give me no game time. I'm not with that shit at all, so I do what they say and ask God to please keep these Officers off my back. To tell the truth it worked---I mean they still fuck wit me just a lil but, all I do is put a smile on my face and do what they say. There is this black girl that work where I work at in the kitchen and she comes to work everyday looking and smelling good. I ain't gone to lie she look good but, I have seen here on them days where she come a lil bit more laid back than others. The days where she come all dressed up she be on point and I don't understand why she don't get alone wit me. Not saying that I need her to so I can try to hollow no, I need her to not have so much attitude so we can work together because wit her having all that attitude all it's gone make me do is make me have attitude wit her. Then she one want to write me up or write me a DR. A DR is when you can go to lock up—so I be saying to myself why do women like this that's pretty be so mean when she can be nice and still get respect and the inmates wont be looking at her like this bitch is nasty ass fuck! Oh well, but then she'll come all dressed up like she going to the club but, all it is she want attention and I don't give it to her. My reason is shhit I can't have you so why am I going to try to be all over you? I do my lil job and be done, then she'll come in all nice and I'll ask her why she be being so mean to me like that. She'll want to play dumb on a nigga…then one day she'll have me cleaning up all kinds of shit. I be like this girl crazy but, I don't say nothing I just say okay and do it so I want get her mad. These inmates that work with me want to see if I'm going to be dumb enough to talk back, get smart with her or say I'm not going to do it so they can see me to jail. You know what I'll do I'll do what she say and I'll tell them she just fucking with me because she want me that's all she's doing lol. I say that just to get their jealous asses mad, I know they jealous of me and could be because they know I'm short and on my way home so they want to see me fuck up! No, no, no buddy I'm way smarter than that. I have kids I have to get back to. This one dude that sleeps in the same dorm with me told me if they be on him like they be on me he would go off. I told that nigga, "Not me." I know the Officers want to see if I'll be dumb enough to get locked up and these fuck ass inmates would love to see me get locked up. I don't give them what they want I give them the opposite but, I wanted to tell dude wit your (dumb ass), "I'm going to keep smiling and keep working, fuck what you are talking about. You done been here three times and all you want to do is see another nigga fucked up because if you didn't you would have told me I did good (Fuck Boy)." You ain't gone do shit if them Officers were on you like that. For one you don't want to go to lock up and for two you don't want to lose your job; so stop it homie! Some days later he gone step to me talking about they called him back to work one day to make some bread; talking about he was gone go off but, he just stayed quite lol yea I know! You wanted to see if you could put in my head that other shit to see if I would do it next time. FUCK NO!

9.27.14

Thinking in Prison

Life---it's what make it or what is dealt to you or you have to make the best of it. I say that to say this, since I have been here in prison a lot has been going on out in the real world. People are coming in or to prison everyday. People are dying out there but, what gets me is it be people I know and it be kind of close, like people I know or someone I use to be with…And all I can do is say, "Bless their soul, Lord Jesus but, also thank you for saving me." I have been in a lot of situations when I was in the streets and I'm only doing 24 months and not only that I'm still blessed to be alive. Its people losing their life everyday out there and it's sad to hear. That's why I can really say thank God I'm here in prison. Not saying this is so safe but, I can say it's safer than being in the streets getting caught up or beefing with these cats over nothing.

Seating in prison really make you think a lot and think about what you don't want to do or be in when you hit the streets again because you can lose your life like that. When I jumped in the streets I never was told how dangerous it was, I just started getting what I thought was easy money until all the shooting and people trying to rob you start to happen. For people that want to get or stay in the streets let me tell you it's not all about the money it's more than getting to the money. From me to you don't get in the streets stay in school and make money that way because let me tell you might no be one of them lucky ones that will make it out without getting a lot of time, getting killed or you having to kill someone yourself. If you done been in jail before, how can you fight it when you're not suppose to have a gun? A lot of the money drug dealers make they either have to pay a lawyer a lot of it, bond out of jail, get robbed and killed for it, or have to go to prison a long time and can't spend the money they made on what the want to spend it on because they have so many years to do. With all them years it's a lot that will happen before that get back home (a lot). If you want to be hard headed and try your luck because you feel like you're tough or maybe a better dealer than the rest then go try it but, you can't say no one never told you don't try it. They say hard head make a soft butt but, I'm telling you the working life is a lot better. It might take longer but, it will make you a lot happier later on in life. Now I'm not saying shit can't happen if your not in the streets too because it do. It can keep you out of a whole lot more trouble by not being in the streets if you keep your mind right. Be wise while you're young and you will have a way better future…I know a lot of drug dealers have a lot and can do a lot but, it's a whole lot that comes with that and if you're ready to deal with going to jail, prison, someone waiting in your house til you and your kids get home because they know you have money. Or they may be sitting in the park-in-lot waiting on you to get out of your car so they run in the house with you with all black on and you don't who it is. They know you and they don't like you so what they do is when they get you in the house they beat you, burn you, anything for you to give up all the money you have then leave you there in your own crib to die…crazy ain't it? This shit real I'm telling you. Yea I did it and I made a lot of money, had a lot of girls but, I wish I would have went a better route. I have no regrets like I say, "God saved me." So I'm here to pass the word.

9.28.14

Thinking in Prison--Words of Wisdom

Working out can be very hard to do some days---boii I tell ya. For me I just cant see myself laying down here not doing nothing but, waiting on my day to go home or waiting to go to chow (It's just not me). I'll feel like I'm just letting time pass right on by and I'm not with that shit at all. Like, I have said before I'm getting older and it's time to really turn up in my life---Meaning keep on pushing and don't just lay down and let the time do me, do the time. Get it out, stay out and try my very best to stay on the right path to accomplish the things I want to accomplish. I can say I do feel good to have goals in life lol but, the scary part is will I accomplish them (I don't know) only time will tell. I can say that I am a person that likes nice things and the only way I can get them and keep them is don't let nothing stop me from the things I'm trying to do. Me being me I want! A lot of times if I start something I will finish it and my plans are to finish my goals and be more in life than a dude that grew up in foster homes and sold drugs. Then went to prison and now you don't see me anymore lol. I'm going to be more than that -- I know a lot of people think he's not going to do nothing, he ain't going to keep going but, let me tell ya'll something the only thing will stop me is Jesus take my life. If I don't happen you will see me in a Bentley chillin wit my kids. I know how I want to live and I know it's going to take a lot of hard work and I'm willing to put in just like my workout. I know sometimes it might get hard but, they say hard work pays off. I know that for a fact because with all the working out I do it's paying off. Even though some days this shit gets hard and I be wanting to quit or not even do it sometimes but, some type of way I end up getting it all done at the end of the day—I can't give up, I want to much shit! So, from me to you if you're on the same page I'm on don't let nothing stop you or get in your way, stay focus and keep going because that day is coming.

10.5.14

Thinking in Prison

A lot of times people speak and don't know what's really going on or try to tell you this or that but, they're not in your situation to know what you are really going through or how you may be feeling. Why you are going through whatever it is you may be going through, so until you walk in my shoes or feel the pain I'm feeling you can't tell me shit! I have this cousin that I thought was really cool when I was younger but, as I got older and still talk with him I started to notice I'm really not like this dude at all. I mean when I was younger it seemed like we was alike but, as time went on I got realer and to me his true side came out. I'm not saying he's just this bad guy all I'm saying is we are different in a lot of ways. I'm in prison so I hit him up just so he'll know that I'm in prison and in my letter I tell him things like, when I was coming up he was like a dad to me. He can send me money if he wants because if he don't have it, I understand. I will just talk to him like any other day like we talked on the streets. I will tell him that I'm good just chillin putting things together for myself like, what I want to do when I get out and some of my plans. When he responded he telling me to worry about myself and nobody else…look you could be right about that but, I also think about other people as well as myself. Not only that I really don't need you to be telling me who to worry about because if you know me you should already know that I'm going to put me first in a situation like this because this is some me time to myself. Tell me some shit I don't know or maybe put me up on some shit you haven't did yet. I feel like since I told him he was like a dad to me back in the days he started to go overboard about trying to tell me what to think about and who to think about. Even though he might or think he's putting me up on game but, wait homie you can't tell a man who to think about and what to think about. I feel like you should be telling him to keep a strong mind and you already know what to do when you get out. The things he's telling me I already know…I guess he want me to think he's really looking out by telling me these things…Not!! So when I tell him he can send me money if he wants to he end up putting a $100 on my books. Now I didn't ask for this I just told him if he wants to it's cool but, if not it's still cool no love lost. I get the $100, I go to canteen and try to get everything at once so I won't have to go stand back in the long line again. I filled up my locker and I managed my food pretty good. Being that he sent me that $100, I'm thinking cuz gone hold me down just a lil bit because I only have like five months left. So rather he sends me anything under that $100 it doesn't matter to me. I'll still save as much as I can because I know he's not a money tree. He has his own family as well. After like three months I hit him up asking him to shoot me something if he can, if not I understand. He shoot me $40 so I hold that down for maybe a month or two then after that I let him know my locker is low can he shoot me something. Now mind you I never ask him to look out for me til I got in a situation like this with me being locked up in prison. Any other time I always have and I only ask for help unless I really need it. So as we're writing each other I talk about other things besides asking for money but, he never pick up on that when he responded. It's always worry about yourself so I be telling him I'm on my shit and I let him in on a lil bit on what I'm going to do when I get out, so he can stop telling me the same old shit. Shhit, I was doing my thing before I even came to prison, so to me you ain't helping me nigga…if you want to help look out while I'm in this bih and stop telling me the same old shit. I can worry or think about who the fuck ever I choose to…hook me up wit a bad lil chick from the 'A' that's how you can help. Send me some flicks on some hoes so I can sell them bitches, that's how you can help me. Nigga I'm in prison I'm learning all I can learn in this bih. I don't need you telling me who and what to focus on. If you were a real nigga you wouldn't be telling me these things, you'll be telling me to keep my head up and don't stress about shit and you'll look out whenever you have it. Not telling me I make you not want to help me because I spent the $100 you sent me. Telling me what the next nigga spent when you was looking out for him. Who the fuck cares what the next dude spent and how he spent it? I don't care…I can't keep that funky ass money when I have to eat. That's what you gave it to me for, shhit you acting like I'm a lil fuckin child like I'm suppose to keep the money for ever or something. What kind of man tells the next man what another man spent when he was in prison? I'm not your child you're just a big cuz and I thought you would understand if I don't have you would be there for me. Not telling me how to spend the money as long as I'm not in here buying tatt's, smoking it up or anything like that. All I'm doing is eating wit the money that's all that matters. Fuck all that other shit you talking about. You don't know what it's like to be in here, fuck what you heard you have to be here to know what's really going on. I can see if I was out in the real world asking this nigga for money then that's different but, I'm locked up I need some help for the first time from you in life. This nigga wants to act like I've been asking for a mil. The prison I'm at is not what you see on TV, this is a work camp and everybody is trying to go home. Also people take liking to all different people and I stay my to myself because its dudes already be hatin. I don't have a lot of time so I stay in my own lane…dudes already know I'm on my shit from the way I workout and they be hatin so hard, it ain't cool to vibe wit them. When you know they are mad because they don't go has hard as you. I'm out there every day working out, no breaks, only sometimes and my reasons is because I know where I want to be and I'm going to have the body to go wit it…I go hard in prison or out. By being in here it help me get my mind right and I came up wit new adventures for my life. So if one of my plans doesn't work fast enough, I can go to the next and also having a nice body you look really healthy, younger and nine times out of ten if you have the right attitude you can pick and choose whatever female you want to. You don't have to settle or for an alright chick, you can go for what you want.

10.10.14

Thinking in Prison

I got a letter from my mom and she was saying in the letter that, she missed me and can't wait for me to get out but, she also said that she don't get to see my kids no more. BOY! You talking about something hurt me within, well that did. For me to feel my momma pain like that it really bothered me on the inside, because I know how much she loves them kids and for my baby momma to not bring them by her house, I know she is hurt. I know she is hurting because she have been there for the kids a long time and for my baby momma to stop bringing them, I know she feel some type of way. I told my mom before don't turn your back on your own son just because you want to be cool with my baby momma and you want to see the kids…Show baby momma how much you love your son and respect him for even bringing the kids into your life. That will show my baby momma that no matter what I love my son and I'm going to be there by his side no matter what (no matter what no body say and show that). But noooo! My mom want to show baby momma more respect than me when I have already put my mom on game about this young lady about her ways and the kids. This girl will turn her back on us whenever her feelings tell her too. So it's cool to show her that woman to woman respect but, if your son is already putting you up on game about this girl don't take a likin to her over your son. You want to show the baby momma that you know your son and that he's a good dad to his kids and you don't want him played with, when it come down to the kids or even your self. Let her know from the jump about how you feel about your son and his feelings. If she do him wrong she's doing you wrong, but nooo momma want to show baby momma a sign of weakness and no respect. So guess what baby momma do she see that and use it against us both. She used my momma against me because she knows my mom is crazy about the kids and will take baby momma side no matter; what just so she can see the kids. Momma doesn't fuckin care because she get to see the kids so she don't care how they do me. As long has they (her and her boyfriend) get to see the kids, they don't care if they see me again. I had been telling my mom that this girl have some nasty ways and she need to back up before she gets hurt…see I already knew she had nasty ways because I lived with her and the kids but, I kept it cool with her as much as possible so I can be around my kids and I will sure we would go by my moms house so she could see the kids. Mom would show that she/we didn't really have that bond that we was suppose to have in front of baby momma. Momma would show her and the kids more respect and favoritism then me. All of us would see it; so to my baby momma that was showing her weakness and also telling my baby momma how could you do your son like this when you know this dude is a good dude lady? Just to see his kids you would turn your back on him in front of his baby momma and kids just so you can get to see the kids, that is fuckin crazy! All this shit is what I'll see but, momma didn't know I would put baby momma up on game on her and her ways. When baby momma seen and when baby momma seen how my mom could be that made baby momma lose respect for her and my reason for doing is because some times I get mad at momma for doing shit like she was doing and being on baby momma side, just so she think she gone see the kids. Her only reason for writing me is because she hadn't been able to see the kids, so now she wishin I was home and she miss me but, nooo you should have did what I told you before. Show baby momma that you love your son no matter if he is right or wrong, if he's right it's even better and I'm not going to let you or anybody come between that. Now if he is wrong I'll let him know but, you still aint finna do him wrong I don't give fuck. If she would have did that and showed my baby momma that I believed baby momma would have had more respect for her. That's why I say if you show any kind of weakness that person would take that and use it against you. My baby momma knew I loved my momma but, she also knew that my mom loved her and the kids more than me or maybe the kids more than me. I came last when they was in the picture but, that wouldn't stop me from taking the kids back over to my moms house. The way I see it is since they know my mom and her boyfriend that's there Grandma and Grandpa. I'm not going to take that from the kids or my mom or her boyfriend. We would still go over there but, all at the same time it made me feel some type of way when I would go over there. Just me not the kids I would let them do their thing but, I knew it would come a day like this and now she needs me to get out so I can try to get the kids back. What she don't know is I'm tired of fighting for kids. I mean when I get out I'll see what's up but, if that shit don't work out I'm moving on with my life. If she wants to take care of them by herself or with her new man go right ahead. It done happened to me before so it ain't no pressure. I'll have more kids my dick still work. I just feel sorry for the kids not getting to see momma them when they are use to seeing them and now my mom feelings are hurt from it. I feel her pain and it makes me feel bad that she haven't seen the kids. I had my cousin call my baby momma cell to ask if she still had my clothes in storage and cuz told me she said yea. So I'm glad I'm still can hit her up when I get out and hopefully something change. I don't know what's going on out there. I haven't heard from baby momma in some months and all of a sudden my mom write me and ask me if I need any money…hell yea I need some money and if she had been sending me money through my baby momma that would have showed my baby momma that my mom won't let me go without no food and she love me and no matter what or way I'm at she is going to be there for me (mom wasn't showing that). It took for my baby momma to not bring the kids around for her to write me, that's what I'm thinking. I mean maybe she do miss me but, I know she miss my kids. The only way for her to get to my kids is to tell me and hope that I get out soon so I can try to get them back in her life. One thing I know is if you show someone or somebody you and another person is strong and have a mad bond they will have mad respect for yall but, if you show that there is weak link they will hate and try there best to play under that/you. I do feel sorry and her pain because I know she love the kids but, she showed a weak link so baby momma will try her and stop bringing the kids whenever she want. Now all momma gone do is look over the bullshit when momma need to make/let her know that the shit she be pulling is not right and she needs to be a real woman and let the kids see their other family members beside hers. It's going to be hard for another/mom that when my mom only shows her bullshit, so it's gone to be hard to get that respect from baby momma…

as for me I'm going to chill, I'm not going to let the shit really bother me, I love my kids and if she want to raise them by herself or with her new man then go right ahead and live a happy lil life and God bless ya'll. I'll just move on and live my life because I have a lot left. Woman try to take you through things to see if they can control you and your feelings, but as I get older I've learned form my past I'm not going to let you push my button, I'll just move on. Maybe, have more kids, but never forget about the kids I already have, but just live my life like they are trying to do…these lil girls want to see a person and not happy because their life was/is fucked up, so what they wanna see if they can make you feel some type of way by doing lil shit. What you do is show them it ain't no pressure, do you baby cause I'm still happy. I'm not going to sweat you at all! You know I'm a good dude if you feel like another dude is better than me then it is what it is, but let the truth be told it's been my pussy for years (Plies)! And those are my three kids you have and they love me to death…so I'm going to sit back and chill, but I'll say this last thing, can't no other man be a more better father to my kids then I! Me and you may not get alone, but when it comes to kids I'm really the best. A lot of times I keep things like this o myself and try my very best to smile, but it seems like I keep on getting tried by these baby mommas, do I stop trying or keep going…fuck it, I'm going to keep going fuck it I love kids.

10-15-14

My brothers, my oldest bruh is laid back. He's two years older than me, but my brother is on the same day… now when we were younger staying with our mom and dad. Mom said, "I use to always be the one to be crying and being stubborn. My older was quiet and liked to play by himself, but I would always go fuck with him and try to get him to play with me, but he would get a lil mad and wanna be by himself. I liked lil cars and he liked lil human dudes to play with, but he wanted his time alone. As we got older and I was able to get him to come stay with me and our younger brother he was kind of the same way still, but all at the same time I still felt like I knew his heart and I can say it was beautiful. One time when we were a teenager we were going to play basketball a dog was after us and bruh was faster than me and we loved to run from dogs because it was fun, but this day the dog was catching up with me and I started to call for my bruh and he turned around and scared the dog off for me. After he scared the dog off I was like wow! but in my head I'm thinking like why in the heck didn't I think to turn around and yell at the dog, but I can I felt loved by big bruh. He was always good at playing sports like basketball and football. All of us would always play sand lock football after school, but it was like big bruh had or would put on this scary look on his face and run right at you if we were playing football or basketball he would jump and shoot good, but as far as being scary he had that on point. I can say I love my brother a lot because he is my oldest brother, but when I look back at our younger days I can't say he was the one that would teach me things. It was like when he learned things he would keep them to himself then show me he could dance or something and I would be looking at him like dang how did you learn that but being that he was in High School and during High School someone was always break dancing and he was able to pick up the moves easy. I mean we danced in Middle School, but I didn't catch on like that at the time because back then when the kids would start to dance and draw a crowd it would look like a fight, so I wouldn't get to see the moves or how they were dancing…back in Middle School I was way in the woods and like I say all we really did back then was work in the fields. It really wasn't no dancing going on where I was, but I can say in other parts of the country, the country boys were and could dance very well. I didn't learn a move or two until I moved a lil closer to the city with our Grandma, but we were still in the country. Before my older brother came to the country with us I don't know if he could already dance or not, all I knew is I would tell him to show me a move or two and he would. I would be looking like dang he can ride out. That's what we called it when we dance, or we would call it bucking and that means ridin' out or break dancing all at the same time, combining moves. Bruh would not show me how to do it, I had to learn it on my own and I did. Another thing is we never would play fight or wrestle it's like he didn't never wanna play with me. Now, me wanting to show my big bruh I was for him and not against him, this dude that stayed down the road wanted to fight, and I didn't care to fight him, so I told my brother and he went down the road, so I could fight dude. It was a pretty good fight between the two of us, but I did that to show my brother that I wasn't scared to fight. I also felt like my brother was missing his other family he was staying with in town but being that I asked him to come live with us he didn't tell us no, but I feel like a part of him deep down was missing his old home. I wanted him to move with us, so we could be closer and get to know each other like brothers should, but as time went on I don't think he cared about that bound with us (his brothers). Being that he was older and stayed with other people he was I believe already doing street things like hanging out late and smoking weed and when he came to the country he found a way to get his weed and hang out with the dudes that did these things. As for me the guys I was around didn't use no drugs at all, all we did was ride to find the girls that's it, no thuggin' at all. One day bruh came home and had a blunt and I asked him can I hit it and I did, but I didn't like it. It made me tired, so I gave it back.

10.22.14

Thinking in Prison

Still in prison, but I can say I am stress free…it feel good to be doing time stress free. You don't have to worry about no girlfriend, no sad news or anything. Just you doing time, that's all. Now, I can think straight and keep on doing me, I don't worry about my kids because I pray for them everything, I don't worry about my mom or brother because I pray for them every night. Not only that I ask myself, "If I was to worry too much what could I do from in here anyway?" (Not a damn thing!) I still feel bless because God is still allowing to live, so that means I still can make it. I can and do get in deep thoughts and the thing is I don't know what it is I be thinking about, I just be thinking. Some days are better than others in here, but for the most I still be chilling. After I shot my moms a letter back it made me feel better telling her don't worry about a thing and I sent her a picture. So, I hope that made her day. I do think about all my kids a lot though, just wishing I was there with them to make them laugh, smile and buy them things boi! Do I get a lil down in here? I think so or maybe not. I do know my moods change everyday, but even when I might be feeling bad I still go outside and workout like it ain't nothing and if my homie out there I still manage to put a smile on and hold a conversation with him, like I been doing okay. Sometimes in here I do get bored as hell if I'm not playing chess or cards because that's what makes time go by. So if I'm not doing one of them I'm looking at TV or on my bed trying to sleep. I been in here trying to keep my mind positive about the things I'm trying to get done when I get out of here. I'm hoping stress don't hit me when I get out because in the real world it can be a lil bit harder, but I do know if God allow me to make it in here I know He will allow me it out there (in the real world). I been working out real hard every chance I get it, gotta look right before I leave prison. They say I done picked up some weight, so I already know when the ladies see me I'm going to be confident and ready to get to know somebody, but I have to get my life on track before I really get into anything. It's a lot that has to be done first.

10.30.14

Thinking in Prison

Woke up this morning thinking about my Moms feelings boi! I know she love all of her boys. I'm one of the ones that she takes a very liking to because I do things to make her happy like laugh and make her feel loved. After I got her letter the other day, it's like I been down and thinking hard every since…before I heard from her I was doing my time pretty good. Now that I have heard from her and the things she have told me like she haven't seen the kids and that she can't wait for me to get out. My time has gotten a lil hard because I'm thinking to much now on what my baby momma got going on out there to where why she haven't taken the kids to see momma or how long has it been since momma seen the kids…damn baby momma be mean to me, but not momma. (Damn!) I wish momma wouldn't have wrote me, I was doing fine. I pray and ask God to please take my pain and her pain away. I know it's about time for me to get out of here and I can say, I do have a plan for my life. I just pray it all work out for me. I dude in here was telling me if someone was to read my book now on how to deal with their problems or how to make it in life they would have to see me succeed. Well, the way I see it is if you are reading my book and seeing where I have came from, where I been and what I'm doing now, you might listen to me or even believe what I am saying. Yes, I know these are the things that have worked for me, but I tell you this, "There is no reason why it won't work for you also." All you have to do is stay strong, but don't forget to ask our God for help. You'll get through whatever it is you might be going through at the time. The hard times will last for how ever long need be, but sooner or later it will be over and the good will come rolling in! Always give God thanks no matter if it's good or bad. Just remember we have to take the good with the bad and still look up and smile and say, "Lord, you know best!"

10.31.14

Thinking in Prison

Sometimes I seat on my bunk or maybe lay down just listening and boi you will hear so much from these dudes. I'm not a fan of jacking my dick, but since I have been here I must say I have not. I'm not into doing that, but with not having sex for a long time and all you do is workout. Your body has to release all of that testosterone, but when I do it I hate it because I feel like I'm molesting myself. To keep it all the way 1000 the only woman I think about when I'm doing it is my last baby momma because that's the last woman I was with before I came to prison. Being the type of dude I am I can't, don't and have not looked at these pics these dudes have here to go back to stall six or seven or let me use their way of seeing it. I don't look at hoes (magazine) and go jack my dick. I just think of my baby momma and get the job done… but some of these dudes just don't mind saying what's on their mind.

When it comes to going back there with the hoes (magazine), fuck that! I want this shit to build up so I can really put this pressure on her, but I can say she is going to have to be very special because I can't give this put up dick to just anybody, just for a nut, fuck that! Yea, when you leave the streets and come in a place like this your mind will roam all over and you think about a lot. Even some times a lot of the women you have been with and sometimes you can smile about it or maybe even have a dream about her. Maybe have a wet dream about her, but if you love that someone a lot of the times your mind will stay on the female and for me that's who I'll jack my dick to. How do I do it? I'll prime him up by calling her name and in my mind I'll think about having sex with her any position I can get that pussy real good. At the same time being that I workout I'm lil aggressive so in my mind I make it like I'm hitting her from the back, something like quickie and bust me a real good nut. Now I'm not knocking the next man on how he do his thing, but my business stay to myself until I get into a conversation and I'll let it be known that I sometimes get the pressure off. It's not an all the time thing for me. Just because some dude next to me has some hoes (magazines) I'm ready to go jack off, fuck that! I sometimes look, but I try my best to keep my mind off sex, but it doesn't work too much. I can say I try and try not to look at the pics because all that's going to do it make me think about having sex when I can't. I just chill and think about how I need to get this paper when I get out. After I make that happen so much pussy is gone come flying my way and guess what I'm going to do make every bit count for the time I've been away thinking it. See when you have more to look for in life you try to think about other things instead of sex all the time because when you get up in age and start having kids, you have to start making plans to do better so they can have it better in life. You have to try and come up with something so you can be able to take care of your kids or family and not be going in and out of prison, because doing so you can lose a lot…your kids get older and you can sometimes lose your girl or maybe your whole famous family all at once, so think it about it all before you go to stall seven.

11.4.14

Thinking in Prison

'Damn!" Back when I had a lil money I never really paid any attention to people hating on you. I guess because I was so busy doing me to where I didn't care, but also to keep it real I might have not known what hating was for some reason. All I seen really was everybody showing me and my homie mad love. No matter way we went, I mean we might get into it with some dudes about who had the nice looking car, but it never ended in no kind of fight or anything like that…now that I'm older and don't have money like I use to it's like I seen so much BS from everybody. Sometimes I seat back and laugh like why are people acting so funny? I mean when everybody found out that me and my home boy wasn't all that cool anymore and I wasn't in the streets like I use to be everybody changed. I guess when you change for the better the dumb motherfuckers stop coming around. My big cousin did tell me, "That once I start doing the modeling/acting I'm going to have to get new friends and a lot of new everything." Now I see what he is talking about, but the thing is I see so much to where I don't want no friends at all. People are so fucking fake it doesn't any sense. The niggas that I use to be cool with, some of them are here in prison with me and them niggas hate harder than a bih. They hate to see you working out and it's not just because you work out hard, it's because they can't do it like you. The other thing is I don't get no visits and I never really go to the canteen line to make like I have so much money. I just chill and be T Dog, that's me. I work out hard because I do have plans with my life and they are thinking I'm suppose to be down worried about the BS. "NOT!" I don't worry about visits because I have to do my time and worrying isn't gone get you no where. Being down isn't gone get me anywhere, so what I do is, do my time and don't let the time do me. I would love to see my kids, but since I haven't I don't get down or worried, I just pray for them and still workout…when I bounce back to the top people gone be saying, "Why you acting so funny." I'm going to say, "You wasn't with me when I was down, you wasn't there when I needed someone to talk to." Where everybody at now that I'm in prison nowhere to be found, but I still keep my head up and still smile. People hate on me like I'm really somebody, I be like what is it about me that make them look at me crazy like they do...then I start to think like they must see Jesus all over me and they are mad because the devil still have them on the BS. See, when you're doing and trying like God wants you to live people don't like that. I mean you might not have a lot, but you are still alive, you still happy and thankful because you know God is still blessing you. He still has your back all you have to do is keep holding on. I know these things about my life, but all at the same time I be like, "Damn, it's like the whole world hate me and I have nobody." Then I start to think like, yes I do because Jesus is always there and things will get greater later. Let me keep real I do be wanting that someone to talk to and that someone to be my true friend, but I can't find that person and when I did try to make a friend in here I started to notice this dude bitch ways. That made me not want to deal with him. Dude is on some real BS talking about what imma do when you leave and stuff like that and in my head I'm like "What you mean nigga, you gone do your time and go home like me." I tell him, "You gone be good homie, you're time is coming just like mine came." This nigga still be down and looking all sad and shit like he wants me to do his time and my time to, I'm not with that shit. I'm trying to be cool with you but, now you want to get in your feelings and hating on me leaving...see that's why I never really let someone in or anybody in because when you bring them in as a friend at first there're cool. When shit isn't going right in their life they want to bring you down with them instead of being happy for you or lifting you up. They rather want to see you fucked up or be down and that's what a lot of the people around me wanted to see with me and since I don't show them that I'm down they try harder and harder. Guess what I do...I just smile! For my baby mommas with my kids holding them back from it's hurting my kids not me.

11.5.14

Thinking in Prison

When you have, people want to be around, people want to help you, people want to love on you, people even want to talk to you, but when you are down them same people don't want to talk. They don't want to be around you and it's almost like you're a nobody. My thing is why look down on me like I'll never come back up, the thing about it is I might be coming up and you might be on your down **'WOW'** or you might be still in that same old spot. While I'm doing the things I told you about before and you didn't want to believe me. Now you're looking to talk and want to be loved on. Wanting that same person you didn't want to be around when he/she was at his down time, now you need all the things he/she was needing…All I'm going to say is, "You better hope that table don't turn." If it do, I'm going to show my ass. I can say I feel good about myself and even though I want more out of life, I'm still working hard to get these things done. The way I see it is there's nothing else to do in life then to live better, become a better person, make your kids smile everyday and make as much money as you can and you know what that will do…make you happy, your kids will be happy, God will be happy because He is the one that's going to make it all possible. Your haters are going to be mad, sad, but respect you from head to toe. When I look around in here (prison) all I see is dudes laying down, talking to each other or smoking all the fucking time or even waiting to eat. I mean you rarely see dudes working out all the time or saying they are working on a plan for when they get out **'No'** all they want to do is lay up and then the ones that work out sometimes they have size. They'll tell you that they gone go hard their last six months, but I'm like have you looked at your belly dude, you need to start now and keep going. They don't be wanting to hear that, but that's why they be hating on me so much because I work out inside, outside and even at work. I get it in; I rather work out then to go to sleep (fuck that). Then they'll say, "You're short (meaning almost to EOS date)". That's why you're working out, but I'm like I have been doing this ever since they let me go to the Rec Yard homie. If I had longer I still want just lay down, I'll be working out trying to think of a better plan to get this money and live better.

11.7.14

Thinking in Prison

I have been down in prison since 12.5.13. I can say I have been getting help from my baby momma #2 and my cousin at times. After some time baby momma fell off. I can say I'm not mad at her because I know she have our kids out there. While my baby momma was helping out when she could I was noticing my mom wasn't doing too much for me during that time. Then after my baby momma fell off here comes mom writing. She sent me some money and 'boi' it makes me feel very good. Not just because I got money but, because she took out the time to write me. She didn't lie about sending me some money because in one of her letters she asked me did I need any money and told me that she was going to send me some…and what do you know! After some days passed, I checked my card and its $100 on it LOL. 'WOW' I'm really proud of her for thinking of her son, 'me'. For her to do what she said she was going to do, that's what's up. When I got her letter and she said she was going to put some money on, I never told myself that she wasn't going to do it. All I said was, "If my mom put some money on my card, she's going to put a $100." All at the same time I didn't want her to put that much on because I'm at my last 60 days and if we get more than $20 within our last 6 months we can't get the $50 they give us when we leave prison. I guess my letter got to her to late for her to know, she did look out. Do I feel loved? Yes… The thing about this all, I was just telling this black dude last night that I was hungry as hell last night and the next my mom hit me with the money. What made me hungrier was last night the cops came in the dorm and shock this dude down and took a lot of his food and he can't get it back. In here when you see someone get shocked down and get their food they hustled for took and you know he can't get it back and you already don't have no food in your locker it makes you even hungrier. All today my right eyes have been jumping and when my right eye jump; to me it means two things. It means God is talking to me; He's telling me that whatever I might be worrying about and thinking about real hard. When my right eye jump the good Lord is telling me don't worry about nothing. He have it all worked out and when my right eye jump it also means something good is going to happen. To me it's like me and God is having our own lil conversation. When my right eye jump it's like God be tapping me on my shoulder and He want to talk to me and that's what I do 'talk!' If my left eye jump I get a lil worried because bad luck. So what I do is when the left eye starts to jump, I start to pray and I ask God to get the devil behind me. It does feel good feeling loved. With my mom sending me letters and money it helps me on how I'm going to feel about when I leave prison about her. It makes me feel loved so it makes me walk with my head up. All at the same time if she had not did what she said she was going to do, I still would have prayed to God and asked Him to help me not be mad at her or no one when I leave prison. I want to leave here with a smile on my face ready for the world and leave the BS behind me. Can't you see how it feels to be loved? It gives you energy, it makes you smile, it also makes you want to show love and when you feel loved you have a different walk about yourself. You just be up lifted and thank God all at the same time.

11.9.14

Thinking in Prison

People say I look too deep into things that go on around me LOL. I think that's 'funny' and the thing about it all the same people that say, "I think too deep" be the same person that be on the BS. The same people that say I be thinking everybody is against me nine times out of ten that same person is one of the ones that is against me because I know! One thing I know about being real, real do real shit. Real say real shit and if a person that feels like or say I look to deep at situations to me I feel like he's trying to hid his hand. He don't want me to notice the BS he's trying to pull on me. He'll tell me I look too deep at shit or I be thinking everybody is against me but, they ain't LOL. "See' to me a fuck nigga and a fake nigga know when they are in front of a real nigga but, when the fuck nigga or the fake nigga is around the real nigga the fuck nigga want the real to think their not against them. That's not the 'case' he is against the real, he just trying to hid his hand. He can't be in a real nigga presence, so he tell the real nigga, "Dawg, everybody ain't against you brah." To me if you're not against me you don't have to speak them words 'homeboy' just talk. I'll know by your conversation and the things you want to talk about if you ain't against me homie, so talk. One thing about a fuck nigga he hate to see someone else go harder than him. He even hate to see or feel like you better than him. If he ever start to feel like this, he have trouble on his hand. He wants to either play under you and what I mean by play under you is, when he get a chance he will make his way to talk about something. Either it's because you getting money, working out or something of that nature. He's only doing that so he can see how much you know and what you know. Now if you know a lot 'oh boi' deep in his heart he gone really hate that but, now if you only know a lil bit then he gone feel like he have you beat. For me I know what I know and a fuck boi ain't going to seat up there and play under me and me not know. I'll be able to tell some kind of way. So I say all of this to say this, "Why would a person look out for you here and there at times and you really don't ask him unless you really need him and then still when you really need him and you still don't be wanting to ask or say anything. So you wait and hold out and 'boom' here he comes with "Brah" you good or are you straight? So you say to keep it real "hell nah" I'm fucked up. He hit you with, "What you need." So you say, "Just this or that" and that person don't mind doing it for you. Now the only reason why this person is doing it for you is because, I'm thinking he wants to be able to say, "Yeah, I use to look out for him when he was down LOL" Me being a real nigga and having a lil finesse game I never let pride get in my way. Since you want to be the big man and try to think you playing somebody. If I'm fucked up and I need something I'll say something to you or wait for you to ask me (then I tell you). Now how I know this person be on the bullshit is because when I tell you I'm going to do something for you; you tell, "Me no you good!" What the fuck is that? If you have been looking out for me when I was down why when I get right and offer to do something for you, you don't want to take it? I do not understand but, you want to wait for me to get out of prison and send you pictures… WTF! Shit don't sound right to me and to keep it real I feel like it's an insult for a person not to take someone's offer. You can't be thinking I don't have it because if I didn't a real nigga want offer at all. He'll just say to himself I'll just wait until I really have it to offer dude something. Not offer and know he don't have it, it don't make no sense…now in some cases a person will offer and it's their last and they just want to show love back from the love you have showed them. My thing is why not take it? If we're trying to be cool I feel like we can lookout for each other not you just looking out for me…when someone is always looking out and don't give someone else a chance to look out sometimes that person that's always getting just might want to keep his hand out and then you done opened a door that might be hard to close. Just know a fuck nigga and a fake nigga is cousins. It's almost as if they think just alike.

11.12.14

Thinking in Prison

Been thinking about all my kids on and off. I try not to think so hard about them but, I guess sometime my mind can't help it. Today I was thinking about my oldest son T Dog Jr. and the things he use to like when he would stay with me. That one thing will be, he use to love 'Swiss Rolls' that was his lil snack. He would want me to keep at my house for him. Today it ran across my mind, like 'dang' I miss my lil man. I mean he's not a lil man no more, he's about to be 13 at the end of the month but, he is still my lil man. When I did use to get Lil T Dog and I would have my Lil friend girl over he would just talk about me all the time. Saying, "My Daddy has this or my daddy has that." I mean everything was 'My Daddy' "My Daddy' and he was right at the time he's daddy did have a lot and 'fuck' child support. When Lil T Dog was with me or he's mom was letting me see him, I would buy him so much and I did that because I love him so much. I remember one time I brought him eight pairs of shoes; four went to my baby momma and four pair stayed at my house. After some time, I guess my baby momma started to feel like she was being to nice by letting Lil T Dog come with me, so she stopped everything. Then put me on child support…but as far as us having fun we had lots of fun. I miss him so much; I miss when he was little and me teaching him how to walk. I miss his smile; I wish I could be the one to have him work out so he'll be ready for whatever sport he wanted to play. It's so much I didn't get to do all because my baby momma don't care if her baby daddies be there because she feel like no matter what her kids gone get token care of. She feel like if she don't have it, it don't matter because if she's not with the baby daddy or get alone with him she ain't gone let him be apart of the kids life anyway. If it comes down to it her dad or mom will help her no matter what or she'll just get some lame ass nigga that probably wanted to be with her in high school but, she didn't want his ass because she wanted he thugs. After being with the thugs and that not working she let the lame in her life and his dumb ass can play daddy to all the kids. Sometimes I be saying, "Dang, I want to have more and more kid." After Lil T Dog I did have more but, it's like I'm going through the same shit with these kids, I'm like "Dang" I don't even know what I want to do. I know now what I should have done from the beginning is wait on the good Lord. When you're living the fast street life a lot of times you never look far ahead at what might happen later. If you and this chic stop talking or liking each other or if you don't have like you use to so how are things going to be if I lose all this. Will she take my child and put me on child support? Nine time out of ten…'she will'. I want more though…just scared because I hate to see kids go through these types of things. My advice to anybody is live your life on the edge, don't plan 'shit'.

    They say the ways of a woman is unknown, and then I say it sounds like it's going to be hard to really love a woman with all your heart because you don't know if she really love you or if she's there for a reason or a season. The thing about it all is I wouldn't mind giving a lot of my heart to that woman that I feel like love me for me and I love her for her…I still have hope because God is my everything!

Thinking in prison

11-19-14

Tristian vs T Dog

Tristian, what it do Tristian? Tristian, ain't nothing just chillin brah. T Dog, yea me too. T Dog, so I see you still in prison. Tristian, yea I'm still here. I see you still in prison too T Dog. T Dog, yea I'm still here homie and I'm thinking about how I'm going to get this money when I get out too. Tristian, what have you came up with? T Dog, shiiiit I wanna do my thing in the streets but being that I know it's a lot of snitching out there it makes me think a lil bit. Tristian well let me say this always go with your first mind gangsta, and it is a lot of telling going on out there so keep on thinking. T Dog, yea yea I know but I still need to get my money up to show everybody that wasn't here for me while I am in prison that I can, and I will come back up and get all the hoes I want. Tristian, let me let you in on something lil brah. The way you are thinking is crazy, you don't have to prove no point to nobody but your kids and what you need to prove to them is you can get out and stay out for them. Your kids are the ones that's going to be missing out if you go back to prison brah and with the way you thinking you headed right back before you know it. T Dog, I hear you but if I get a lil street money I can take care of my kids with the money I make. Are you thinking about that Mr. smart guy? Tristian, of course I am brah. I know you must take care of your kids, but you also have to be smart and make better decisions, so you want to be in and out of prison. You know that rap song when dude say it isn't about who bread the longest it's about who can stay out on the streets the longest because one slip then you out of here. Tristian, if that's your shit then you better listen to the words real clear lil brah. It's other ways to get money out in the real world. Think of some of things you like to do. T Dog, things I like to do that's funny. Brah the things I like to do is, get fast money, fuck bad bitches and leave the house when I want and don't have to worry about clocking in to no fucking job. Tristian, I feel you on that but selling drugs can take a lot from you if you go back to life. I mean if you ask me you bless to be doing 24 months and as many times you done been to jail and this your first to prison you bless all you must do is, why you in prison think of something you like to do other then selling drugs and laying on your ass and whatever you come up with be good at it. I think your very smart dude and I know you can come up with something that you can do to get money. T Dog, brah I really can't come up with nothing, I mean I never sat down and thought about what I'm good at besides getting females. I mean I never liked school coming up so going to collage is a no to me but wait I did go to massage school and learn how to do the massage part, but the school work was hard to me, but the hands-on part was a lot easier. Tristian, well that's a start. You don't think you will ever want to go back? T Dog, I might want to because in prison I've learned some things I can go to school for and learn about it and maybe like it, but I don't know yet and plus I have been writing a book about my life and the things I have done in life and all of this is in one book. Tristian, well sounds good so far and I see you can come up with something you can do besides sell drugs. Writing is good. Do you like writing? T Dog, no I'm just doing it because it helps pass time but to keep it real, the things I have been thought I know someone else have been thorough wordster or maybe something just like what I have been through and my book is a book that can help someone to know how to pray, keep his head up and never stop trying in life no matter what you have been through something like a motivational book because I like to help people that maybe feeling down, ya feel me? Tristian, yea I feel brah. It's good you are doing what you are doing with the book and if you get that book published you never know how much it will help someone and not only that it could bring you in a lot of money. So, it sounds like you on a good start so far. T Dog, I'm wanting to come up with a clothing line using my name, what you think? Tristian, I think that's a good ideal just do your homework and get out and make it happen. T Dog, yea, but a lot of this is going to take money to get everything started, so what you think I need to do to get the money to get it going? Tristian, not sell drugs. When you get out go look for a job. Think about it if you find a nice lil job and you save up some money and stay prayed up I bet God will bless you with everything you need T Dog. T Dog, boi Tristian you one positive dude man and o guess it's good so I'm going to try it all out and see what happen. Tistian, T Dog, to keep it real positive is always a better way to go bro, I mean people might think it's lame but when your positive it's better and plus it makes God happy. The way I see it is I tried the street life and I can't lie it had fun times and some bad, but I want to try something different, so I'll be pleasing God because through it all he is the one that always had my back from the day I was born all the way till now. So, I'm going to do something to make him happy and not just think of me and what my flesh want's. what I'm saying is I also want you to do this with me T Dog it will make things a whole lot easier for the both of us, you feelin me brah? T Dog, yea I'm feeling you brah. T Dog, everything you been saying is so right and true and I want to be apart of what you are doing. Tristian, you can be and to keep 1000 I'm going to still need you because o like your swag. T Dog, that's what's up brah, I'm all in then and I'm going to try my very best to do the positive and the right thing, so we can make God smile and be happy for us and continue to bless us. Tristian, ok! Tristian, well folks I have a friend with me on what I'm trying to do in life and T Dog said he's going to try so with we out. Thanks to everyone for reading my book. I hope it have touched you all in many ways and don't forget to keep God first and you'll never be last.

11.22.14

Thinking in Prison

Still been thinking a lot, I try to stay busy as much as I can so I don't have to think that much, like if I'm at work I'm busy making sandwiches. So my mind be on getting a job and what I'm going to tell the people at the job, "What kind of work I know how to do," It's been a long time since I have had a real job and the only real job I have had that I have to go to and be to is the one in prison. We have to go to work here or we will go to the box. The box is 'lock up' and I don't want to go there. Besides it makes your time longer for you to go home. Being at work makes me feel like I have a real job. Plus it takes my mind out of my feelings and thinking about things that want to make me feel some type of way. Working out takes my mind off a lot too! When I'm working out a lot of times I'm outside and being outside it's like your mind can go so far, because even though you're behind a fence you still can look up and all around you to take your mind to a more positive state of mind. 'See' in prison you have to have a strong mind or you won't last long. It's like if you let a lot of the BS mess with you or things you can't change it can mess with your mind. That's something I don't want, because it's nothing out there I can do or change while you are doing time. It's best to stay stress free and think about as much positive as you can. One of my favorites that keeps me from stressing is my Daily Bread. It puts my mind at ease when I read each page. The thing about it is, it touch home about everything. I mean it's positive but, it's not so positive and ways to where it seems unreal. It makes you think a lot, in a good way though! It keeps you on the right track, the right state of mind and it helps a lot. I make sure I read it every day. Reading my Daily Bread will be one of the things I take with me when I leave prison. I'm going to keep on reading and not only do I read my daily bread I pick up my Bible and have Bible study by myself, so I can fellowship with what I have been reading; that's a lot of fun! The Lords will, I'm going to read my Daily Bread to my kids and whoever else that wants to listen. A lot of times when people are in the real world (free) a lot of times some people don't take out the time to pick up their Bible to read Gods word. Some of us wait till we get locked up to find God. I can say this, "A lot of times being locked up can and do save our life." God be 'knowing' and a lot of times He puts us in paces like prison to see if we will search for him or will we just do our time, get out and think everything is all good. A lot of times a lot of people do their time and get out but, what's ahead is unknown to them. They either get killed or they even might have to keep coming back and neither one is one that I'm going to want to have to do. The people in the real world be feeling like they are doing so good and God is saving them to where they don't take out the time to pick up the word or go to church. The only time they do these things like, pick up their Bible or go to church is when something wrong happen in their life. To me at least being in prison will give a person a wake up call and a chance to think better or his/her life so they can get out and do better but, always remember that God comes first and never forget that. 'Yea' we might get in a lil trouble here and there and have to go to prison but, it also be an eye opener for a lot of us so we can do better and think better. Always thank God for everything, the good and the bad. It's a reason for everything! To all: Always feel like you are special to God no matter if you understand or not, no matter if you may feel like this or that person don't love you. 'Always know' that there is 'someone' that love you. You might not be able to see Him but, he is there with us everyday we wake up and go to sleep. We are special to God and He wanted me to tell ya'll this.

11.25.14

Thinking in Prison

"Damn." I wanna feel loved. It's crazy how all these people in the world and all the people I have been friends with, all the people I know and all the females I have talked to ain't here to show me a friendly love. Sometimes I try to think of why not. Why don't anybody care that I might be all alone, sad or maybe even down at a time like me being in prison? When you doin time 'boi' people act like you never was there for them or you never was in the picture, why? I don't know myself; all I know is when my brother and homeboy was locked up! I was there sending them pictures and writing them and when both of them got out they didn't care to be around me. My brother, before he got out he called me on the phone telling me that we were going to hang out and be around each other so we can get closer, well that damn sho' didn't happen. After he got out, at the time I was smoking weed and I went all the way to the city to get him with no driver license and he gave me $200 to put in my pocket. I guess he was trying to give me some money back after I got him the lawyer, so he wouldn't have to do ten years. After we got to our moms house we smoked and then after a few weeks he started to do his own thing. That was him going back to the hood to do the same thing to put him in prison like the first time. Me…all I wanted to do was smoke weed and work out and that's what I kept doing. I didn't let anything get in my way from working but, my brother wasn't with it. He had other plans and those same plans landed him back in prison for four more years, after being out for no more than a year. All I can say is, "I wish I had a real friend or brother but, everybody leaves." My old best friend we was writing each other a lot while he was in prison, I was sending him pictures and 'all'. My only reason why I ever sent him my money was because somewhere in my heart I knew he wouldn't keep it all the way real with me when it came down to it. I mean even when we use to be together all the time and calling each other brothers, he still wasn't keeping it 100 with me. I look pass a lot of it just because the love I grew to have for him. When he got out of prison he came and gave me a hug but, after I guess he heard I was out the streets he didn't want to be cool with me anymore is what it seemed. After seeing him in the gym other reasons came out because why he is doing his own thing (I won't get into all that). When he was locked up I stayed writing him and telling him how much I missed him, how I couldn't wait for him to get out and when he got out he acted like I'm a dude that never said a word to him. The 'ladies', I already know what it is and was. At the time, Tristian/T Dog was living his life. The streets were my old lady, so at the time I wasn't ready for a relationship. All I ever wanted was to do me and live my lil life LOL. I know a lot of ya'll wanted to be with me or even have a baby from me. It didn't happen for many reasons and a lot of the times I can admit it might have been my fault but, I'm not saying I'm sorry. All I'm saying is, "I understand!" Ya'll ain't wrong for living ya'll life now. Ya feel me? 2 Timothy 1:12 Jesus love me and all of us, so in the end that's all that really matters.

11.29.14

Thinking in Prison

    I don't know if I've talked about this or not but, I was telling this guy this today that sometimes I feel like I don't like to be shown love. My reason for that is because sometimes a way a person love is indescribable. Not saying it's all bad, I guess the way a person might love you sometimes in some cases you might not understand their love, how they love you or how much. They have their own way of showing their love and to me that is kind of scary. I 'my self' like to be the one to love and show love because in my eyes in some way I feel like or know what I do is from the heart, not saying theirs ain't. It's just you might not understand theirs. I feel like love makes you weak…only if you let it. When you don't get love it feel bad but, it also make you go hard and work hard at everything you are trying to do. Now it do feel good to be loved or feel loved but, like I say it can try to attack your mind so your mind will get lazy on you. I'm not saying my love is all 'that' because I'm not perfect but, I will say my love is real and be from the heart. Being in prison it's good to do time alone, that way you stay away from getting hurt or someone hurting you. I'm not saying if you have someone to be there for you or wanna be there for you to not let them. What I'm saying is it can hurt if they stop out of the blue for whatever reason if your mind ain't strong to deal with them stopping. When you are free in the real world try your best to do good because a person or people will always remember the good. If you ever be down they will find it in their heart to make sure you have or get something and if you're in prison something is better than nothing. They may not show love the whole bid but, if they show it every now and 'then'…then you're doing 'good'. 'Now' for me it backfired on me just a little bit but, all at the same time the people I was around that seen me show love to this or that person. When I'm down they try their best to be there for me because they know when I had it they showed loved. So even though the person I showed love to didn't show love back, God always put in someone else heart to show love to me. So, I'm still not 'losing'…do good and it will come back to you, do bad and bad will make it way back to you. I guess I'm saying there's a 'right' and a 'wrong' way to love somebody - like Keith Sweat say.

11.28.14

Thinking in Prison

I been writing a book about my life and I try to go back and read some of the things I've wrote and I'll start reading a lil bit, but as I'm reading some of it kind of makes me feel some type of way…so I'll have to put it up. I guess I be getting in my feelings when I start to read some of my pain. Then I might pick up a page that is pretty cool and laid back and I can read all of that and all I can do is smile. I started writing about my life the beginning of the years and being writing ever since and have not stopped. After writing about my life it do feel a whole lot better to have how I was, how I been and how I'm feeling now that I have a lot of very most of it off my mind and off my heart onto a piece of paper. It's a relief off me and that's why it's hard for me to go back and read most of it. The thing about it all is, I'm going to have to go back and type it and also check for a lot of misspelled words. I'm not to that part yet, that won't come until I get out. The good part about it, it's gone and I don't have to look back no more. All I'm going to do is focus on what's going to be ahead being that I'm changing a lot of my old ways and I feel like a better man now, so to me all I see is better days. I must say having hard times is what makes you a better person. You either change for the better and have better or stay the same old person and continue to keep having those bad days. Now, if you're bad days started when you were young then that's something you can't help until you get up in age to do something about it. From me to you or whoever don't let your past stay with you too long, you know why? Because you can miss out on your blessings and you don't need or want that. Keep this in your head, God made us go through the things we went through so we could share with someone else and also find Him and call on Him for help. That is His reason for doing it or letting it all happen. Don't be upset or mad too long, ya feel me? Say to yourself, "**Trouble doesn't last always.**" Always try to be better, never stay the same, and always try to see where you can improve at about yourself. In life it will get hard, but it won't stay forever because God loves us.

12-21-14

The Mind of Tristian

Real love is pain, so I won't give up. Real nigga all day so I know imma come up.

I never let a person in so easy, you never know what they have on there mind, they could be out to get you, they could be out to wanna be like you or better then you, but imma say this. God only made one of me, so you can pretend or try to be like me, but deep down you can't be better then me. "I" can only be me that's why God made just one of me:} and I'm thankful! All I need is God there for me because he will never turn his back on me or anyone, anybody else he loves. Love is a hurting thing and people want to love you for many different reasons and when they feel like you love you them back that's when they want to play with your heart, all because they want to be better then you or want your spot. So, they play right up under a person to get to know them well and then they go for the "kill" lol. It's funny to me because you still can't win like that. God see everything, so you might be being a snake to me but not to God and I'm a child of God and he is watching over me! May God bless you!

12.27.14

Thinking in Prison

It's close for me getting out of prison and while I'm in here I noticed a lot more haters. I try my best to cool as much as I can. A lot of the dudes that know I'm getting out either be mad, hating or in their feelings. That makes me stay away from a lot of the dudes in here, because with me always feeling like they're hating on me leaving, shit can get real. I still do my time like go in the TV room or play chess, but most of the time I just seat back and watch other people play. The shit talking that some of these guys be on I really don't be on. I like to play a nice lil game without the name calling, shiit that's how I see them play on TV. To me that's how I wanting to play, unless you're talking trash like brah you ain't gone type shit. Not "No nigga' this and "Nigga that" and snatching the pieces off the board like you feel some type of way about me or something. Then I don't wanna play because deep in your heart you want to fight me is the way I feel. Since you have no reason or have the heart to step to me, you think you can or try to beat me in chess. The thing about it all I have gotten better since I been playing, so beating me ain't all that easy. Other than that I been cooling though. I been writing this so-called movie I have and I let one or two people read some of the pages and so far so good. They feeling it, so to me that's a "plus." I just have to finish it, al I been doing is while I let one or two people read it I been letting my mind brain-storm, so I can come up with more to write about so, it won't fall apart and start to be boring. I just fall back and chill a lil bit. Another thing in here I noticed is people only want to be cool with you when you have money and bring in a big bag of canteen. That's when they want to slide up under you and want to talk and try to be so cool with, but if they feel like you are broke they stay away. So you know what I say, "Money brings fake friends." A lot of these dudes hate on me because I think I stay in my own lane. I don't be seating around asking any and every dude in here, can I have this or can I have that? If I don't have, I don't have. If I fuck with you and I may need something then I'll ask, if not I'll fall back. People don't like that, they think a person think they are all that if you fall back. Guess what, I let them get mad because if I don't have it then I don't have it. If I want it and I fuck with you then I'll come ask you, but most of the time if I don't have I just chill and thank God when I don't have and praise Him when I do have. A lot dudes in here just be sitting around bullshitting with themselves. Some of the other dudes they don't seat somewhere and try to think of something, so they want have to come back to prison. All they want to do is smoke, play cards, play with each other and hate on the next man because they see him doing his one two. Ya feel me? I let them hate because I don't give a fuck. Shiit, I want to be rich if I can be and I still want they bitch ass to keep on hating and watch me count up. So I can point the finger at they ass and laugh and smile…and have that look on my face like "Ya, bitch I told ya I was gone get right." It seems or shall I say, "Being that I'm broke I see a whole lot more than when I had it." To me it's good because when I come back up people gone think I'm acting different because I'm not gone be fucking with them. I'm going to be in my own lane doing positive things and being around people that's trying to have something in life or around people that already have. I can say that what I have noticed about myself is that I look at life a lot different too. I feel like a lot of my bad ways have changed to good and my good just have gotten better. I know I'm going to respect women a lot better than I did and that's about the only thing I needed to better about myself. Other than that I'm just going to better as much as I can. To all the women who feel like I disrespected them I'll tell you this, "**I am sorry.**" I was young and came up with an attitude because of what I have been through and that made me be disrespectful if anybody got me mad, so I hope ya'll understand and forgive me.

12.31.14

Thinking in Prison

When I write I speak from the heart. Like I have said before is your real mom and dad may have not been there for you at times or may not have been there for you when you was younger but, to me I think that your real parents (some) of them really care about you or their kids. For me, I went and found out what it was that had me and my brothers left in foster care. Like I might have said before, I'm not mad because the good Lord knew what He was doing for my mom and her kids. 'Yes' we ended up in foster care, 'yes' we ended up with diffent families but, I'm going to say this, "I do love my real mom." I'm so thankful that God has kept her alive after all the drug use she done. To me it's a blessing for her to be a Grandmother to my kids and for me to see it with my own eyes. Even give them nicknames is a blessing and for us to come and be back around each other. Yeah, I do get mad at her at times but, when I think about her and the fun we have had 'boi' it makes me feel so good to have a mom I can go to her house, laugh with her, talk to her about almost anything, take pictures of her and bring the kids I have in her life to make her even more happy. I'm even thankful to be able to make her mad and my reason sometimes for that is because I be wanting her to feel our pain. I do believe that if she was better off in life things would have been different. For me, I would have been a mommas boy but, in a very "G" way, meaning liking to keep my mom happy and have as much fun with her. Not having woman ways that ain't me "T Dog. While I have been here in prison I feel like I have became a better man. I thank God that I'm here and thank God that I have been through the things I've been through because it made me the man I am today. It also showed me that the love that I have for my mom is deep and I becoming a better person will make her even happier, to see one of her sons that come fuck with her do better things in life and make something out of himself instead of just a street nigga. See, I have been a street nigga and I see everything that comes with it. I know God saved me when I was in the streets and you know how I know he saved me? Is because I've been to jail 49 times and this is my first time ever in prison. While I was in the streets people done tried to rob me at my house and I acted crazy while fighting them off and they don't shoot me. I know He love me because I'm still here, I have all my teeth, I still can work out hard, I'm in good shape, my mom is still her, all of my kids are still alive, my brothers are still alive and 'guess what' I am 'thankful.' I love the Lord so much for loving me like He does. It feels so good to be one of His chosen ones. My homie asked me, "If I was to die today would I go to heaven?" I told him, "Yea, I'll go to heaven." How I know is, is because I feel like my heart is right and I try my very best to do right. God know that I'm not perfect but, He also know that I'm a good dude and I try. I know He want us to at least try to do better and that's what I be doing 'trying'. After all the things I have seen or been through I still don't have hate in my heart. I don't hate my mom, I don't hate my brothers, I don't even hate my baby mommas for not bringing my kids to see me while I have been here in prison. As a matter of fact I still pray for them and ask God to bless them and make them happy if they ain't happy. I already know that they ain't happy because they are trying to make me unhappy by keeping the kids all to themselves, when they know that ain't right. They know that the kids should be with their real dad instead of a step dad or some other dude. I'm still happy though, I know God is going to work everything out for me and my kids. It feels good knowing their God that seat on high and sees you and hears your heart crying for help and happiness. Out of the blue He gives it to you. While I have been here in prison I have been showed loved by the ones that know me and the ones that don't know me. It's all because of the good Lord. A lot of people have died out there while I have been here in prison and I feel sorry for them. When I start to think I just start to count my blessing and thank God for keeping me alive. For my foster mom, I love you too and I know we had our good times and the bad. I'm thankful to have lived with you. I love the family very much and always will. Martha, Toya and Valentine I love ya'll so much because ya'll really fuck wit T Dog. I'm so thankful to say that we are family. To the rest of the family ain't no hard feelings, to Grandma, you did good! To my big cousin, Lil Jerome even though you don't understand what it's like to be a inmate in prison and you done made me mad with some of the things you have wrote me, I can still say, "I love you my nigga." You have been there for me in the hard times and to me that really counts.

The mind of me..T Dog aka Tristian…I was thinking prison was a place that's hard core or something but all I been seeing at this place where I'm at is straight bullshit. Dudes that's from your same city ya'll might speak when ya'll first see each other but after some time past you start to notice how dude look at you and it damn sho don't be in a good way…niggas from your same city will hate on you or just hate you because he know you from the city and you is or was the type of nigga that got money, fucked a lot of hoes and stayed in your own fucking lane and now that ya'll are in prison together and you still on the same shit he start to notice your ways. You stay to yourself, but I guess when you get in prison shit is supposed to change…fuck no homie it isn't dat

I hate or dislike you but if I didn't fuck with you then I don't fuck with you now. It isn't no hard feeling but not only I can see it in your eyes how you feel about me, so I stay away before it gets ugly. Niggas from your same city will want to go though it with you before a nigga you don't know want to go though it with you. It's crazy to me because from what I was told from the dudes in my county jail they was saying when you get to prison niggas from your same city call you they homeboys but they know damn well they dislike a nigga but I already knew that shit was not going to be like homie from the county was telling me …one thing about niggas they want to see you down or hurting and doing bad, or trying to be down with them and if you ain't on that type of time/ shit they mad because they can't talk about you…rule#1 keep niggas out of your game room. One thing about me ill speak and even hold a conversation with you but I'm a real nigga so that mean I am not going to sit there and try to be all in your face like I want to be so cool with you, that's not me. I been cross before and I never want to be crossed again…it's not that I'm scared of no nigga I just like to stay to myself as much as possible that way I stay away from the bullshit, get money and don't have to worry about somebody telling on me or hating on me that's close to me…that know things about my life and try to use them against me later in life. Not that I have so much to hide but staying to yourself is the best—talk to people that's going to help you in life. Don't just waste time talking to because time is money unless you in prison like me and the only person you can be cool with is the person you cant learn shit from all you can do is listen to his life story but I have learned over the time that no matter how smart you might be that the person you think isn't all that smart if you sit back and listen you might be able to pull something out of the conversation. I've said before I really don't like people, but I know I'm not in this crazy world by myself, so I must deal with them but deal with them in different ways. See I just can't see myself hating on the next man because I'm too busy doing me. I really can't see myself worried about what the next man is doing unless I'm trying to get money like him because if it isn't about money or putting me up on some Real Shit I can really care less.